MW01069749

Easy Indian Cookbook

A Simple Asian Cookbook for Preparing
Tasty Indian Foods

By
BookSumo Press
All rights reserved

Published by
http://www.booksumo.com

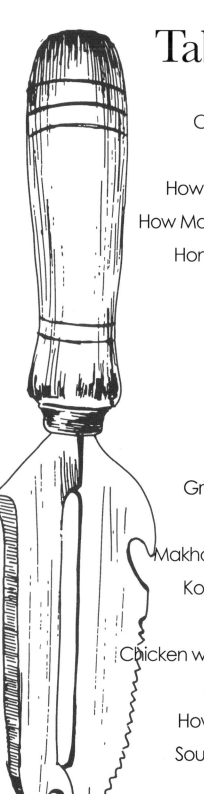

Table of Contents

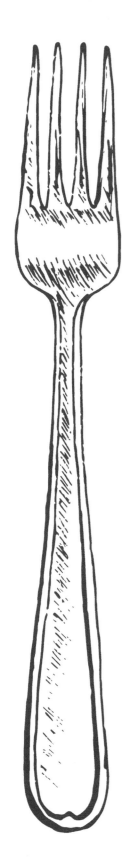

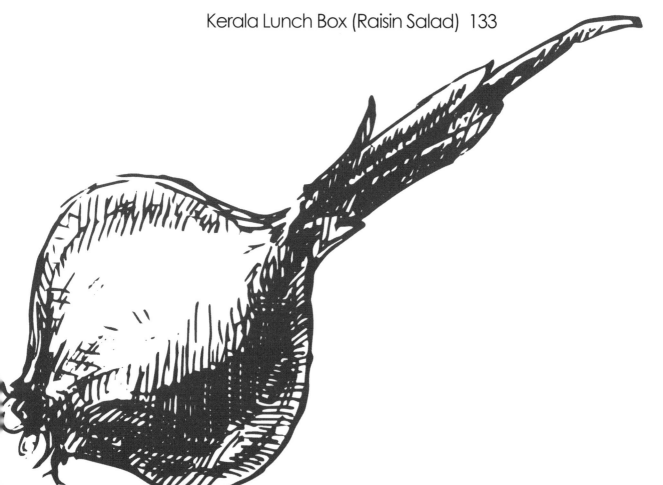

Lentils
Masala

Prep Time: 15 mins
Total Time: 50 mins

Servings per Recipe: 4
Calories	361
Fat	4.9
Carbohydrates	0
Protein	554
Cholesterol	63.7
Sodium	16.9

Ingredients

1 tbsp olive oil
1 large onion, minced
6 cloves garlic, minced
2 pinches red pepper flakes
1/2 tsp ground turmeric
1 1/2 tsp garam masala
1 C. lentils

4 C. vegetable broth
2 sweet potatoes, peeled and cut into 1/2-inch cubes
4 C. chopped fresh spinach
salt to taste

Directions

1. In a large soup pan, add the oil over medium heat and cook until heated through.
2. Add the garlic and onion and stir fry for bout 3-5 minutes.
3. Add the garam masala, turmeric and red pepper flakes and stir fry for 1-2 minutes.
4. Add the broth and lentil and cook over high heat until boiling.
5. Now, set the heat to low and simmer, covered for 15-20 minutes.
6. Add the cubed sweet potato and cook until boiling.
7. Now, set the heat to low and cook, covered for 10-12 minutes.
8. Stir in spinach and salt and cook for about 4-5 minutes.
9. Serve hot.

CURRIED
Cauliflower Skillet

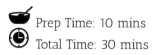 Prep Time: 10 mins

Total Time: 30 mins

Servings per Recipe: 4
Calories   220
Fat   11.2
Carbohydrates   0
Protein   641
Cholesterol   27.6
Sodium   5.5

Ingredients
3 tbsp canola oil
2 tsp cumin seeds
1 tsp caraway seeds
1/2 red onion, chopped
4 cloves garlic, minced
1 head cauliflower, cut into florets with
1-inch stalks

1 large potato, diced
1 tsp red chili powder
1 tsp ground turmeric
1 tsp salt
1/4 C. chopped fresh cilantro

Directions
1. In a pan, add the oil and heat over medium heat.
2. Stir in the caraway seeds and cumin seeds and stir fry for about 1-2 minutes.
3. Add the garlic and onion and cook for about 8-10 minutes.
4. Add the cauliflower, potato, turmeric, chili powder and salt and mix well.
5. Now, set the heat to medium-low and simmer, covered for 18-20 minutes, mixing as required.
6. Serve with the garnishing of the cilantro.

Kebabs
Bazaar

🥣 Prep Time: 15 mins

🕐 Total Time: 2 h 25 mins

Servings per Recipe: 8	
Calories	304
Fat	22.6
Carbohydrates	76
Protein	665
Cholesterol	4.7
Sodium	20.1

Ingredients

2 lb. lean ground lamb
2 onions, finely chopped
1/2 C. fresh mint leaves, finely chopped
1/2 C. cilantro, finely chopped
1 tbsp ginger paste
1 tbsp green chile paste
2 tsp ground cumin

2 tsp ground coriander
2 tsp paprika
1 tsp cayenne pepper
2 tsp salt
1/4 C. vegetable oil
skewers

Directions

1. Add all the ingredients except the oil into a bowl and mix until well combined.
2. With a plastic wrap, cover the bowl and place in the fridge for at least 3 hours.
3. Take 1 C. of the meat mixture and mold around a metal skewer in the shape of a sausage, pressing slightly.
4. Repeat with the remaining meat mixture.
5. Arrange the skewers in a large baking sheet and place in the fridge before cooking.
6. Set your grill for high heat and generously, grease the grill grate.
7. Cook the kababs onto the grill for about 10 minutes, flipping occasionally.
8. Remove from the grill and serve hot.

HOW TO MAKE
Garam Masala I (Tandoori Style)

 Prep Time: 5 mins
Total Time: 5 mins

Servings per Recipe: 5 tbps
Calories	19 kcal
Fat	0.8 g
Carbohydrates	2.9g
Protein	0.7 g
Cholesterol	0 mg
Sodium	4 mg

Ingredients
2 tbsps ground coriander
1 1/2 tbsps ground cumin
1 tsp garlic powder
1 tsp ground ginger
1 tsp ground cloves
1 tsp brown sugar

1 tsp ground fenugreek
1 tsp ground cinnamon
1 tsp ground black pepper
1 tsp ground cardamom
1/2 tsp ground allspice

Directions
1. Get a bowl, and evenly mix or sift: allspice, coriander, ground cardamom, cumin, black pepper, garlic powder, cinnamon, ginger, fenugreek, brown sugar, and cloves.
2. Get a good container that is airtight and store your mix.

How to Make
Garam Masala II (Karachi Style)

Prep Time: 5 mins
Total Time: 5 mins

Servings per Recipe: 2/3 C
Calories	24 kcal
Fat	0.7 g
Carbohydrates	4.1g
Protein	0.8 g
Cholesterol	0 mg
Sodium	6 mg

Ingredients
1/4 C. black cumin seed
2 large bay leaves, crushed
2 tbsps green cardamom seeds
1/4 C. black peppercorns
1 1/2 tsps whole cloves

1 tbsp fennel seed
4 cinnamon sticks, broken
1 pinch ground allspice

Directions
1. Toast the following in a skillet for 11 mins: cinnamon sticks, cumin, bay leaves. Fennel seed, cardamom, cloves, and peppercorns.
2. With your grinder or mortar and pestle process the spices into a fine powder and store in your favorite container.

HOMEMADE
Curry Spice Mix

Prep Time: 15 mins
Total Time: 16 mins

Servings per Recipe: 13 tbps
Calories   13 kcal
Fat   0.5 g
Carbohydrates   2.3g
Protein   0.6 g
Cholesterol   0 mg
Sodium   25 mg

Ingredients
2 tbsps smoked paprika
2 tbsps chili powder
2 tbsps curry powder
2 tbsps ground cumin
2 tbsps garlic powder, or more to taste
2 tsps ground turmeric
2 tsps ground cardamom
2 tsps ground coriander
2 tsps onion powder

1 tsp dry mustard
1 tsp fennel seeds
1 tsp garam masala, or more to taste (use a previous recipe)
1/4 tsp rubbed sage
salt and ground black pepper to taste
1 pinch ground ginger (optional)

Directions
1. Get a bowl and sift the following into it, in order: ginger, paprika, black pepper, chili powder, salt, curry powder, sage, cumin, garam masala, garlic powder, fennel, turmeric, mustard, cardamom, onion powder, and coriander.

2. Store in an air container if you have one.

Chicken Tikka
Masala

🥣 Prep Time: 30 mins
🕐 Total Time: 2 hr 20 mins

Servings per Recipe: 4
Calories	404 kcal
Carbohydrates	13.3 g
Cholesterol	143 mg
Fat	28.9 g
Fiber	2.5 g
Protein	24.6 g
Sodium	4499 mg

Ingredients

1 cup yogurt
1 tbsp lemon juice
2 tsps ground cumin
1 tsp ground cinnamon
2 tsps cayenne pepper
2 tsps freshly ground black pepper
1 tbsp minced fresh ginger
4 tsps salt, or to taste
3 boneless skinless chicken breasts, cut into bite-size pieces
4 long skewers

1tbsp butter
1 clove garlic, minced
1 jalapeno pepper, finely chopped
2 tsps ground cumin
2 tsps paprika
3 tsps salt, or to taste
1(8 ounce) can tomato sauce
1 cup heavy cream
1/4 cup chopped fresh cilantro

Directions

1. Take lemon juice, yogurt, two tsps cumin, cayenne, cinnamon, ginger, black pepper, 4 tsps of salt and add into one mixing dish (possibly a big bowl).
2. Add the chicken to the marinade, cover it, and place it in a refrigerator for one hour.
3. Preheat a grill or frying pan to its highest heat.
4. Add chicken to skewers and throw away the marinade.
5. Add some butter or nonstick spray to your grilling grate.
6. Place the chicken on the grill and allow it to cook until its juices are clear. The approx. time is equal to about 5 minutes on each side.
7. Take your butter and place it into a big skillet or wok. The skillet or wok should be placed over medium heat.
8. For about one minute stir fry (sauté) some garlic and jalapeno.
9. Take some paprika and cumin (approx. 2 tbsps each), and also three tsps of salt and add

these ingredients to the garlic and jalapeno.

10. Grab some cream and tomato sauce and place the two ingredients on low heat and continually stir the contents until they become thick. This process should take about 20 minutes.

11. Combine everything with your grilled chicken and let everything cook for an additional ten minutes.

12. Plate your contents and add some cilantro as a garnish.

13. Enjoy.

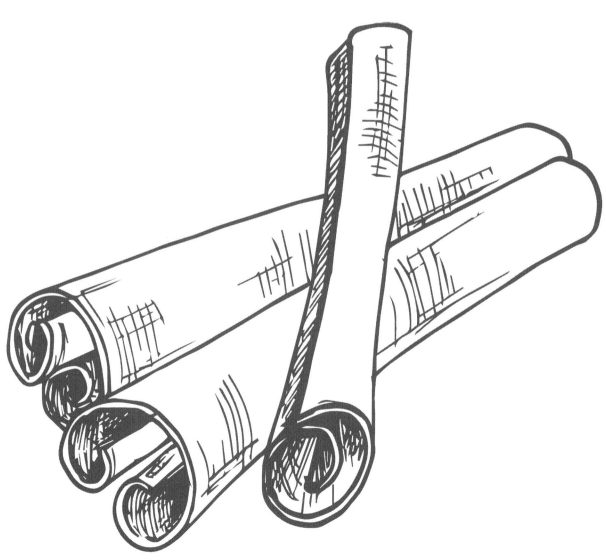

Aloo
Phujia

 Prep Time: 10 mins

Total Time: 30 mins

Servings per Recipe: 4 to 6
Calories	235 kcal
Carbohydrates	25.7 g
Cholesterol	0 mg
Fat	14.1 g
Fiber	4 g
Protein	3.3 g
Sodium	593 mg

Ingredients

1 onion, chopped
1/4 cup vegetable oil
1 pound potatoes, peeled and cubed
1 tsp salt
1/2 tsp cayenne pepper
1/2 tsp ground turmeric
1/4 tsp ground cumin
2 tomatoes, chopped

Directions

1. Grab a frying pan or skillet to begin. Add some oil to your skillet and begin to brown some onions.
2. Once onions are nicely brown season them with the following: cumin, salt, turmeric, and cayenne.
3. Combine with the seasoning your potatoes, and cook everything for at least ten mins. Make sure that you are stirring consistently as you do not want your seasonings to burn.
4. After ten mins has elapsed, mix in tomatoes and allow everything to cook until the potatoes are soft.
5. The pan should be covered and the cooking time for this step is about ten mins.
6. Allow everything to cool.
7. Serve.

MY FIRST
Korma

Prep Time: 20 mins
Total Time: 1 hr

Servings per Recipe: 4
Calories	398 kcal
Carbohydrates	13.4 g
Cholesterol	95 mg
Fat	27.5 g
Fiber	2 g
Protein	25.3 g
Sodium	477 mg

Ingredients

1/4 cup cashew halves
1/4 cup boiling water
3 cloves garlic, peeled
1(1/2 inch) piece fresh ginger root, peeled and chopped
3 tbsps vegetable oil
2 bay leaves, crumbled
1 large onion, minced
1 tsp ground coriander
1 tsp garam masala
1 tsp ground cumin

1 tsp ground turmeric
1 tsp chili powder
3 skinless, boneless chicken breast halves - diced
1/4 cup tomato sauce
1 cup chicken broth
1/2 cup heavy cream
1/2 cup plain yogurt
1 tsp cornstarch, mixed with equal parts water

Directions

1. Grab a small container and combine the boiling water with cashews. Allow this mixture to sit for about 20 mins.

2. Get your food processor ready for work. Add garlic and ginger inside the processor and work the contents until they become a paste. Once the contents are a paste set it to the side.

3. Grab a skillet or wok and add some oil and get it nice and hot with some medium heat.

4. Add your bay leaves to the oil and let it cook. Bay leaves should fry for about half of a minute.

5. Now you should add some onion to the oil and fry them down until translucent (three to five mins).

6. Get your food processor contents (ginger and garlic) and combine it with the onions and let everything fry for five minutes.

7. Combine with the mixture the following seasonings: chili powder, coriander, turmeric, masala, and cumin.

8. Combine your chicken with the seasoning and fry it for five minutes. Now combine your chicken broth as well as your tomato sauce. Make sure that you cover this pot, and lower the temperature.

9. Let everything slowly simmer for 15 mins. Make sure to stir the contents every once and a while.

10. Grab that food processor again and throw in some cashews and their accompanying water into the food processor with some yogurt and cream. Mix it all together until paste like.

11. Now take your food processor mixture and combine it with the chicken let everything cook for another 15 mins.

12. Finally combine the cornstarch and let everything go for an additional 2 mins.

13. Let food cool.

14. Plate it. Serve it. Enjoy it.

MASOOR
Daal

Prep Time: 5 mins
Total Time: 35 mins

Servings per Recipe: 4

Calories	185 kcal
Carbohydrates	25 g
Cholesterol	0 mg
Fat	5.2 g
Fiber	9.7 g
Protein	11.1 g
Sodium	868 mg

Ingredients
1 cup red lentils
1 slice ginger, 1 inch piece, peeled
1/4 tsp ground turmeric
1 tsp salt
1/2 tsp cayenne pepper, or to taste
4 tsps vegetable oil
4 tsps dried minced onion
1 tsp cumin seeds

Directions
1. First step when dealing with lentils is to clean them. So run the lentils through water until the water runs clear.
2. Grab a sauce pan and place your clean lentils in it with the following seasonings: cayenne pepper, ginger, salt, and turmeric.
3. Take all these ingredients and submerge them in water inside of your sauce pan. Get everything to nicely boil. Make sure that you remove any foam which manifests during the boiling process.
4. Lower the temperature and let the contents simmer. Make sure you stir everything every once and a while.
5. Let the food simmer until the lentils are nice and soft and everything looks like a soup.
6. Grab a container that can be put in the microwave. Inside of the container place the following things: cumin seeds, oil, and dried onion.
7. Set the container in the microwave on the highest setting for 45 secs.
8. Get the onions to a brown like color but make sure to not burn them.
9. Take out the microwave contents and combine it with the lentils.
10. Plate, serve, enjoy.

Spinach
Dhal

🥣 Prep Time: 10 mins
🕐 Total Time: 40 mins

Servings per Recipe: 4	
Calories	362 kcal
Carbohydrates	44.9 g
Cholesterol	15 mg
Fat	13.4 g
Fiber	18.3 g
Protein	21 g
Sodium	693 mg

Ingredients

1 1/2 cups red lentils
3 1/2 cups water
1/2 tsp salt
1/2 tsp ground turmeric
1/2 tsp chili powder
1 pound spinach, rinsed and chopped
2 tbsps butter

1 onion, chopped
1 tsp ground cumin
1 tsp mustard seed
1 tsp garam masala
1/2 cup coconut milk

Directions

1. First step is to take your lentils and put them in a container filled with water for about 20 minutes (soak everything).
2. Grab a large pan, add some water, and boil it. Once the water is boiling combine the following ingredients: chili powder, salt, turmeric, and lentils.
3. Now you need to cover the pot and get it boiling again. Once you have the pot boiling immediately turn the temperature down to get a nice simmer going.
4. You want everything to simmer for approx. 15 mins. Now add your spinach to the simmering goodness and let it simmer and cook for another five mins. At this point you should notice your lentils are nice and soft (if not continue simmering). Remember to add more water if you think it is needed.
5. Grab another pan. This time a smaller one.
6. Place the new pan over medium heat and combine the following ingredients: mustard seeds, melted butter, cumin, and onion. Make sure that you are stirring this mixture constantly.

7. Cook everything down until the onions are transparent. Once you find that your onions are transparent combine the mixture with the lentils from earlier.
8. Finally combine lentils with coconut milk, and garam masala.
9. Heat everything for a few more mins (2 mins).
10. Let contents cool.
11. Plate and enjoy.

Chicken
Tandoori I

Prep Time: 50 mins
Total Time: 1 day 45 mins

Servings per Recipe: 4
Calories   356 kcal
Carbohydrates   13.7 g
Cholesterol   102 mg
Fat   18.8 g
Fiber   3.3 g
Protein   35.6 g
Sodium   734 mg

Ingredients

2 pounds chicken, cut into pieces
1 tsp salt
1 lemon, juiced
11/4 cups plain yogurt
1/2 onion, finely chopped
1 clove garlic, minced
1 tsp grated fresh ginger root

2 tsps garam masala
1 tsp cayenne pepper
1 tsp yellow food coloring
1 tsp red food coloring
2 tsps finely chopped cilantro
1 lemon, cut into wedges

Directions

1. Grab your pieces of chicken and begin to take off the skin.
2. For each piece of chicken you want to create a slit or cut from the top to the bottom.
3. Get a non-deep dish and add some salt and lemon juice to the chicken pieces. Making sure to cover everything.
4. Allow everything to marinate for at least 20 minutes.
5. Grab some yogurt, onion, garlic, cayenne pepper, ginger, and masala, and combine everything in one nice sized bowl.
6. Combine and stir the contents until smooth. Add some yellow and red food coloring (or skip if you do not care for non-natural ingredients)
7. Combine the yogurt based mixture with the chicken and allow it to marinate in a fridge for at 6 hrs. But an entire day is ideal (24 hr).
8. Get an indoor grill grate or an outdoor grill and set to a medium heat level and coat it with oil or nonstick cooking spray.

9. Place the chicken pieces on the grill and let them cook until the middle is no longer pink.
10. Remove from grill and garnish with lemon pieces and cilantro.
11. Plate and enjoy.

Grilled Chicken
Tandoor II

🥄 Prep Time: 10 mins
🕐 Total Time: 8 hr 55 mins

Servings per Recipe: 8

Calories	349 kcal
Carbohydrates	5.4 g
Cholesterol	120 mg
Fat	20.5 g
Fiber	1.1 g
Protein	34.2 g
Sodium	618 mg

Ingredients

2 (6 ounce) containers plain yogurt
2 tsps kosher salt
1 tsp black pepper
1/2 tsp ground cloves
2 tbsps freshly grated ginger
3 cloves garlic, minced
4 tsps paprika

2 tsps ground cumin
2 tsps ground cinnamon
2 tsps ground coriander
16 chicken thighs
olive oil spray

Directions

1. Get yourself a medium sized container for mixing the following ingredients: ginger, yoghurt, cloves, salt, pepper, and salt (a bowl would be ideal).
2. Also combine the following taking care to mix all the contents together evenly: coriander, garlic, cinnamon, paprika, and cumin.
3. Set this mixture to the side to settle and move on to the next step.
4. Grab your chicken and clean it under some water (ideally cold water).
5. After the chicken has been cleaned. Dry it with napkins or paper towels (apply a patting motion for best drying results).
6. Now you want to take your chicken and mix it with the yogurt mixture we made earlier. In a large plastic bag that is reseal-able. Make sure that after you have added the chicken and yogurt to the bag you remove all the air which will be trapped inside.
7. Work the bag by turning it upside down and shaking it lightly to evenly dispense mixture and cover all the chicken.
8. Put this bag of chicken in a container and place it in the fridge for at least 8 hours (ideally

you would allow this to marinate overnight) reposition the bag occasionally (not necessary but recommended).

9. Get your grill ready. Set it to a medium level of heat and cover the grate with oil or a nonstick cooking spray.
10. Remove each piece of chicken from the bag and spray it with olive oil. Place it on the grill.
11. Allow each piece of chicken to receive direct heat for 2 minutes.
12. Then turn each piece of chicken and allow for direct heat for another 2 mins.
13. Move each piece of chicken to the side of the grill and let it receive indirect heat for at least 25 to 35 mins and make sure the internal temperature of the meat is at least 180 degrees Fahrenheit.
14. Remove from grill, plate, and serve.
15. Throw away the remaining seasoning left over in the bag.

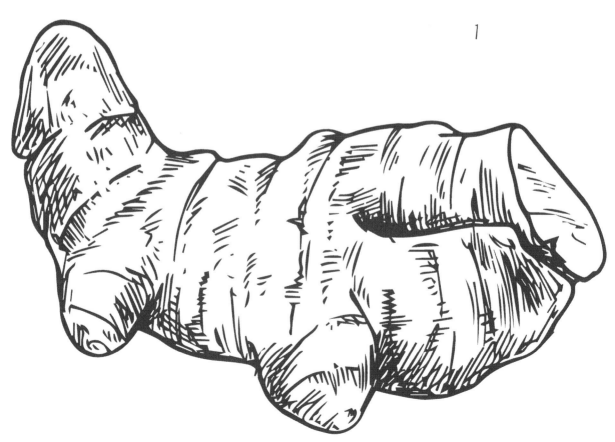

Chicken
Biryani

Prep Time: 30 mins
Total Time: 2 hr 30 mins

Servings per Recipe: 6 to 8	
Calories	832 kcal
Carbohydrates	78.9 g
Cholesterol	134 mg
Fat	35.1 g
Fiber	5.1 g
Protein	47.8 g
Sodium	1522 mg

Ingredients

4 tbsps vegetable oil
4 small potatoes, peeled and halved
2 large onions, finely chopped
2 cloves garlic, minced
1 tbsp minced fresh ginger root
1/2 tsp chili powder
1/2 tsp ground black pepper
1/2 tsp ground turmeric
1 tsp ground cumin
1 tsp salt
2 medium tomatoes, peeled and chopped
2 tbsps plain yogurt
2 tbsps chopped fresh mint leaves
1/2 tsp ground cardamom
1(2 inch) piece cinnamon stick
3 pounds boneless, skinless chicken pieces cut into chunks
2 1/2 tbsps vegetable oil

1large onion, diced
1pinch powdered saffron
5 pods cardamom
3 whole cloves
1(1inch) piece cinnamon stick
1/2 tsp ground ginger
1pound basmati rice
4 cups chicken stock
11/2 tsps salt

Directions

1. Okay let's begin this recipe by grabbing a frying pan or large skillet and mix in some veggie oil (two tbsps).
2. Once our veggie oil is hot add potatoes and fry them until they are a brownish color.
3. Once the potatoes are brown remove any excess oil and place them to the side for work later.
4. Keep the pan hot and add two more tbsps of oil and add some garlic, onion, and ginger.
5. Cook these contents until you find that your onions are nice and soft and slightly brown.
6. Now we want to add the following ingredients to our onions for seasoning: tomatoes, chili,

salt, pepper, cumin, and turmeric.

7. Make sure that you vigorously stir the seasonings to protect them from burning while frying for about five mins.

8. Now we want to combine the following ingredients: a cinnamon stick, yogurt, cardamom, and mint.

9. Once these ingredients are added we want to place a lid over the pot and lower its heat to the lowest level.

10. Take care to stir the mixture every once and a while until you find that the tomatoes have been turned into a pulp.

11. You may notice that the mixture will become dry and sticky. If this is the case you will need to combine some hot water to the cooking pot occasionally.

12. Once the contents are thick. Grab your chicken pieces and combine them with the sauce.

13. You will want to make sure to mix the chicken well with the sauce so that every piece is evenly coated.

14. You now want to place a lid on the mixture and lower the temperature to its low level.

15. The chicken should be heated at this level while covered until you find that it is tender. Typically this will take about 35 to 45 mins.

16. Cook the chicken down until you notice a bit of gravy left. If you find that the gravy is too much remove the lid from the cooking dish for a while and let the contents continue to cook.

17. Now let's get to the rice.

18. Get your rice and wash it until you find the water running clear. Drain the water with a colander and let the rice sit aside for about thirty mins.

19. Now grab a large frying pan or skillet and add some veggie oil with some onions and fry it up until it is nice and golden.

20. Grab the following ingredients and add them to the onions: rice, saffron, ginger, cardamom, cinnamon stick, and some cloves. Make sure that you stir consistently until you find that your rice is completely covered with spice.

21. Now we need to get another pot of a medium size.

22. Grab some chicken stock as well as some salt.

23. When you find that the rice is nice and hot you want to add this chicken stock and salt to it. Make sure that you combine everything well.

24. Now let's grab that chicken and potato pot from earlier.

25. We want to combine the chicken and potatoes nicely into the rice mixture.

26. Cover the rice pot with a lid and make sure it is completely sealed. We now want to take the temperature down to its lowest level and let this rice simmer for about 20 mins.

27. Make sure that you do not lift the lid while it is cooking.

28. After 20 mins has elapsed remove the lid and fluff the biryani.

29. It is now ready to be plated and served.

30.   Enjoy.

MAKHANI
(Indian Butter Chicken I)

Prep Time: 10 mins
Total Time: 35 mins

Servings per Recipe: 4
Calories   408 kcal
Carbohydrates   15.6 g
Cholesterol   107 mg
Fat   27.8 g
Fiber   2.2 g
Protein   23.4 g
Sodium   620 mg

Ingredients

1 tbsp peanut oil
1 shallot, finely chopped
1/4 white onion, chopped
2 tbsps butter
2 tsps lemon juice
1 tbsp ginger garlic paste
1 tsp garam masala
1 tsp chili powder
1 tsp ground cumin
1 bay leaf
1/4 cup plain yogurt
1 cup half-and-half cream
1 cup tomato puree

1/4 tsp cayenne pepper, or to taste
1 pinch salt
1 pinch black pepper
1 tbsp peanut oil
1 pound boneless, skinless chicken thighs, cut into bite-size pieces
1 tsp garam masala
1 pinch cayenne pepper
1 tbsp cornstarch
1/4 cup water

Directions

1. Grab a saucepan (as large as possible) and heat it over medium heat.

2. Take some onions and shallots and stir fry them until they are soft and see-through. Combine onions and shallots with the following ingredients: one bay leaf, some butter, chili powder, one tsp of garam masala, ginger-garlic paste, lemon juice, and cumin.

3. For approx. one minute the ingredients should be stir fried.

4. For approx two more minutes continue to stir contents consistently and add some tomato sauce, some yogurt, and finally some half and half cream.

5. It is important that you continue to stir the mixture for an additional 10 minutes over low heat, letting it simmer.

6. Add some salt and pepper and place the cooking pot to the side away from the heating source.

7. Take another skillet and add one tbsp of oil over a medium level heat.

8. Add some chicken to your heated oil and cook it for about 10 minutes until it is lightly brown.

9. Grab some garam masala (1tsp) as well as some cayenne (same amount) and add it to the chicken, reduce the heat.

10. Combine 3 tbsps of sauce with the chicken and simmer the contents until your chicken is no longer pink.

11. Once the chicken is fully cooked (i.e. no longer pink) add it to the sauce.

12. Combine some water and cornstarch and mix it with the sauce. Allow everything to cook for an additional five to ten minutes, until it is thickened.

13. Plate, serve, enjoy.

KORMA
Vegetarian Edition

Prep Time: 25 mins
Total Time: 55 mins

Servings per Recipe: 4
Calories	462 kcal
Carbohydrates	41.3 g
Cholesterol	82 mg
Fat	31 g
Fiber	8.4 g
Protein	8.6 g
Sodium	1434 mg

Ingredients
11/2 tbsps vegetable oil
1small onion, diced
1tsp minced fresh ginger root
4 cloves garlic, minced
2 potatoes, cubed
4 carrots, cubed
1fresh jalapeno pepper, seeded and sliced
3 tbsps ground unsalted cashews
1(4 ounce) can tomato sauce

2 tsps salt
11/2 tbsps curry powder
1cup frozen green peas
1/2 green bell pepper, chopped
1/2 red bell pepper, chopped
1cup heavy cream
1bunch fresh cilantro for garnish

Directions
1. Grab your oil and add it to a skillet or frying pan. Skillet should be set over medium heat.
2. Combine with oil, some onions, and let it cook until completely translucent. Next you should combine: garlic and ginger.
3. Let the new mixture of cooked onions, garlic, and ginger, cook for approx. one minute.
4. Grab some carrots, cashews, potatoes, and tomato sauce, and combine them all with some curry powder and salt for seasoning.
5. Allow everything to cook for approx ten mins. taking care to stir consistently. Make sure that your potatoes are tender before moving to the next step.
6. Take the following ingredients and stir them into your current mixture: peas, green and red bell peppers, and cream.
7. Simmer everything for about 10 minutes on low heat.
8. Plate your dish for serving.

Chennai
Relish

🥣 Prep Time: 5 mins
🕐 Total Time: 4 hr 35 mins

Servings per Recipe:	24
Calories	38
Fat	0.1
Carbohydrates	0
Protein	2
Cholesterol	9.6
Sodium	0.2

Ingredients

2 red bell peppers, chopped
1 sweet onion, chopped
1 C. white vinegar
1 C. white sugar
1 tbsp crushed red pepper flakes

Directions

1. Add all the ingredients in a medium pot and stir to combine.
2. Place the pan over medium heat and bring to a boil.
3. Now, set the heat to low and simmer for about 30 minutes, stirring often.
4. Remove from the heat and transfer the relish mixture into a bowl.
5. Keep aside to cool slightly.
6. Place the bowl in fridge for at least 4 hours or for the whole night.
7. Serve with your favorite dishes.

CHICKEN WITH TOMATOES
South Indian Style

Prep Time: 25 mins
Total Time: 2 hr 15 mins

Servings per Recipe: 6
Calories   134
Fat   5.4
Carbohydrates   57
Protein   547
Cholesterol   6.9
Sodium   14.7

Ingredients
1 large onion, chopped
4 cloves garlic, chopped
1 slice fresh ginger root
1 tbsp olive oil
2 tsp ground cumin
1 tsp ground turmeric
1 tsp salt
1 tsp ground black pepper
1/2 tsp ground cardamom

1 (1 inch) piece cinnamon stick
1/4 tsp ground cloves
2 bay leaves
1/4 tsp ground allspice
6 skinless chicken thighs
1 (14.5 oz.) can whole peeled tomatoes, crushed with liquid

Directions
1. In a food processor, add the ginger, garlic and onion and pulse until smooth.
2. Place a large frying pan over medium heat and heat oil in it.
3. In the hot oil, add the onion puree and stir fry for about 12 minutes.
4. Add the bay leaves, cinnamon, allspice, cardamom, cloves, cumin, turmeric, salt and black pepper and mix well.
5. Then, stir fry for about 3 minutes.
6. Add the chicken thighs and mix well.
7. Cook for about 5 minutes, stirring frequently.
8. Add the tomatoes and mix well.
9. Set the heat to low and simmer for about 2 hours, stirring as required.
10. Enjoy.

Mumbai
Yellow Rice

Prep Time: 5 mins
Total Time: 25 mins

Servings per Recipe: 6
Calories   154
Fat   4.1
Carbohydrates   10
Protein   418
Cholesterol   26.1
Sodium   2.5

Ingredients
1/8 tsp powdered saffron
2 C. boiling water, divided
2 tbsp butter
1 C. uncooked long-grain white rice
1 tsp salt

Directions
1. In a bowl, add 1/2 C. of the hot water and saffron and stir until well combined.
2. Keep aside for about 15-20 minutes.
3. Add the butter in a pan over medium-high heat and heat until melted completely.
4. Add the rice with salt and stir fry until aromatic.
5. Add the saffron water and remaining hot water and cover the pan.
6. Now, set the heat to low and simmer for about 20-25 minutes.

HOW TO MAKE
Basmati Rice

Prep Time: 10 mins
Total Time: 45 mins

Servings per Recipe: 6
Calories	216
Fat	5.4
Carbohydrates	0
Protein	394
Cholesterol	38.9
Sodium	3.9

Ingredients
1 1/2 C. basmati rice
2 tbsp vegetable oil
1 (2 inch) piece cinnamon stick
2 pods green cardamom
2 whole cloves
1 tbsp cumin seed

1 tsp salt
2 1/2 C. water
1 small onion, thinly sliced

Directions
1. In a large bowl of water, soak the rice for at least 25-30 minutes.
2. In a pan, add the oil over medium heat and cook until heated completely.
3. Stir in the whole spices and sauté for about 1 minute.
4. In the pan, add the onion and cook for about 10 minutes, stirring frequently.
5. Strain the soaked rice completely.
6. In the pan, add the strained rice and stir fry for about 1-2 minutes.
7. Stir in the water alongside the salt and let the mixture cook until boiling.
8. Now, set the heat to low and cook, covered for about 15-20 minutes.
9. Remove from the heat and keep aide, covered for about 5 minutes.
10. Uncover the pan and with a fork, gently fluff the rice.
11. Serve immediately.

South Indian
Curried Shrimp

Prep Time: 15 mins
Total Time: 30 mins

Servings per Recipe: 4
Calories	416
Fat	32.1
Carbohydrates	146
Protein	930
Cholesterol	10.9
Sodium	23

Ingredients

2 tbsp peanut oil
1/2 sweet onion, minced
2 cloves garlic, chopped
1 tsp ground ginger
1 tsp ground cumin
1 1/2 tsp ground turmeric
1 tsp paprika
1/2 tsp red chili powder

1 (14.5 oz.) can chopped tomatoes
1 can coconut milk
1 tsp salt
1 lb. cooked and peeled shrimp
2 tbsp chopped fresh cilantro

Directions

1. In a pan, add the oil over medium heat and cook until heated completely.
2. Stir in the onion and sauté for about 4-5 minutes.
3. Remove from the heat and let the onion cool for about 2-3 minutes.
4. In the pan of the onion, stir in the ground spices, ginger and garlic and place over low heat.
5. Stir in the coconut milk, can of tomatoes and salt and simmer for about 10 minutes, stirring as required.
6. Now, add the shrimp and gently, stir to combine.
7. Simmer for about 1 minute.
8. Stir in the cilantro and serve hot.

CHICKEN
Curry 101

Prep Time: 20 mins
Total Time: 45 mins

Servings per Recipe: 4
Calories	313
Fat	21.7
Carbohydrates	38
Protein	268
Cholesterol	14
Sodium	19.1

Ingredients
3 tbsp olive oil
1 small onion, chopped
2 cloves garlic, minced
3 tbsp curry powder
1 tsp ground cinnamon
1 tsp paprika
1 bay leaf
1/2 tsp grated fresh ginger root
1/2 tsp white sugar

salt to taste
2 skinless, boneless chicken breast halves - cut into bite-size pieces
1 tbsp tomato paste
1 C. plain yogurt
3/4 C. coconut milk
1/2 lemon, juiced
1/2 tsp cayenne pepper

Directions
1. In a pan, add the oil over medium heat and cook until heated through.
2. Stir in the onion and stir fry for about 4-5 minutes.
3. Add the ginger, garlic, bay leaf, sugar, curry powder, paprika, cinnamon and salt and stir fruy for about 1-2 minutes.
4. Now, stir in the chicken, coconut milk, yogurt and tomato paste and mix well.
5. Let the mixture cook until boiling.
6. Now, set the heat to low and cook the curry for about 20-25 minutes.
7. Add the cayenne pepper and lemon juice stir to combine well.
8. Cook for about 4-5 minutes.
9. Remove from the heat and discard the bay leaf before serving.

Curried
Chicken Pizza

🥄 Prep Time: 20 mins
🕐 Total Time: 9 hr

Servings per Recipe: 4
Calories   1058
Fat   65.8
Carbohydrates   159
Protein   2444
Cholesterol   64
Sodium   53.7

Ingredients

1/2 C. tandoori paste
6 tbsp plain yogurt
2 skinless, boneless chicken breast halves
6 tbsp olive oil, divided
4 pieces tandoori naan bread
3 tsp spicy curry powder
1 tsp ground turmeric

1 yellow bell pepper, thinly sliced
1 large red onion, thinly sliced
4 (4 oz.) spreadable goat cheese
1 tomato, thinly sliced
4 oz. feta cheese

Directions

1. In a large glass baking dish, add the yogurt and tandoori paste and beat until well combined.
2. In the baking dish, place the chicken breast haves and mix with the yogurt mixture generously.
3. Refrigerate, covered for at least 8 hours.
4. Set your oven to 400 degrees F.
5. In a pan, add about 1 tbsp of the oil over medium-high heat and cook until heated completely.
6. Remove the baking dish from the refrigerator and transfer the chicken breast halves into the pan, shaking off the excess marinade.
7. Cook for about 9-10 minutes flipping the chicken breast halves often.
8. With a slotted spoon, transfer the chicken breast halves onto a plate.
9. With 2 forks, shred the chicken breast halves.
10. Spread 1 tsp of the oil over each naan bread evenly, followed by the curry powder.

11. In the bottom of a baking sheet, place the both naan breads and cook in the oven for 5 minutes.
12. Meanwhile, in a frying pan, add the remaining oil over medium-high heat and cook until heated completely.
13. Ad 2 tsp of the curry powder, turmeric, onion and bell pepper and cook for about 6-7 minutes, stirring frequently.
14. Remove the vegetable mixture from the heat and keep aside.
15. Remove the baking sheet from the oven.
16. Top each naan bread with layer of the cheese, followed by some curry powder, chicken, onion mixture, tomato, remaining feta cheese and a pinch of curry powder.
17. Cook in the oven for about 20 minutes.

Crepes
Chapra

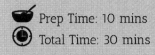 Prep Time: 10 mins

Total Time: 30 mins

Servings per Recipe: 6
Calories	125
Fat	5
Carbohydrates	41
Protein	41
Cholesterol	16.5
Sodium	3.5

Ingredients
1 C. all-purpose flour
1 C. water
1 egg
2 tbsp butter, melted
1 pinch salt
1 tbsp caraway seeds

Directions
1. In a bowl, add the water and flour and beat until well combined.
2. In the bowl of the flour mixture, crack the egg and mix until well combined.
3. Add the butter, caraway seeds and salt and beat until well combined.
4. Add 1/4 C. of the flour mixture into a heated non-stick skillet into an even circle and cook for about 2-4 minutes.
5. Carefully, change the side of crepe and cook for 30 seconds more.
6. Cook the remaining crepes in the same way.

SWEET MASALA
Chicken Tenders

Prep Time: 15 mins
Total Time: 40 mins

Servings per Recipe: 4	
Calories	426
Fat	13
Carbohydrates	73
Protein	377
Cholesterol	55.8
Sodium	24.9

Ingredients

1 lb. chicken tenders, cut into bite-size pieces
2 tsp garam masala
1 tsp garlic powder
salt and black pepper to taste
2 tbsp olive oil
1/2 yellow onion, finely diced
1 1/2 C. chicken stock

1 C. apricot preserves
1/4 C. white vinegar
1 tsp hot pepper sauce
1 tsp lime zest
1 tbsp butter

Directions

1. In a large bowl, mix together the garlic powder, garam masala, salt and black pepper.
2. Add the chicken pieces and toss to coat well.
3. In a pan, place the oil over medium heat and cook until heated completely.
4. Add the onion and stir fry for about 4-5 minutes.
5. Stir in the chicken pieces and stir fry for about 5-6 minutes.
6. With a slotted spoon, transfer the chicken mixture into a bowl an keep aside.
7. In the same pan, add 1 C. of the stock and cook until boiling, stirring to scrape the bottom with a wooden spoon.
8. Add the vinegar, apricot preserves, hot sauce and enough broth and stir until sauce becomes smooth.
9. Stir in the cooked chicken and cook for about 10-12 minutes.
10. Add the butter and stir until melted completely.
11. Remove from the heat and serve with a garnishing of the lemon zest.

Curried
Almonds Pilaf

Prep Time: 5 mins
Total Time: 55 min

Servings per Recipe: 6
Calories	404
Fat	11.1
Carbohydrates	20
Protein	257
Cholesterol	72.5
Sodium	6.6

Ingredients
1/4 C. butter
1 onion, diced
1 1/2 C. pearl barley
1/2 tsp ground allspice
1/2 tsp ground turmeric
1/4 tsp curry powder
1/2 tsp salt

1/8 tsp ground black pepper
3 1/2 C. chicken broth
1/4 C. slivered almonds
1/4 C. raisins

Directions
1. In a pan, place the butter over medium-high heat and cook until melted completely.
2. Stir in the barley and onion and stir fry for about 4-5 minutes.
3. Add the broth, curry powder, turmeric, allspice, salt and black pepper and stir to combine well.
4. Cook until just boiling.
5. Now, set the heat to low and cook, covered for about 35-40 minutes.
6. Remove from the heat and with a fork, mix in the raisins and almonds.
7. Serve hot.

SAMOSA
Pies

🥣 Prep Time: 20 mins
🕐 Total Time: 1 hr 25 mins

Servings per Recipe: 6

Calories	248
Fat	6.9
Carbohydrates	< 1
Protein	176
Cholesterol	41.3
Sodium	6.5

Ingredients

Crust:
1/2 C. all-purpose flour
1/2 C. whole-wheat pastry flour
1/4 tsp salt
2 tbsp vegetable oil
6 tbsp ice-cold water
Filling:
1 1/4 lb. potatoes, peeled and quartered
1 tbsp black or yellow mustard seeds
1 tsp curry powder
1 tsp ground ginger
1/2 tsp ground cumin

1/8 tsp red pepper flakes
1 1/2 tsp vegetable oil
1 C. diced onion
1/2 C. diced carrot
1 tbsp minced garlic
1 C. low-vegetable broth
1 C. frozen peas
2 tsp white sugar
salt and ground black pepper to taste
2 tbsp milk

Directions

1. Set your oven to 375 degrees F before doing anything else.
2. In a large pan of the slate boiling water, cook the potatoes, covered over medium-low heat for 15 minutes.
3. Meanwhile, for the crust: in a bowl, add the salt and both flours and mix well.
4. Slowly, add 2 tbsp of the vegetable oil, beating continuously until well combined.
5. Slowly, add the cold water and mix until a dough ball is formed.
6. With a damp tea towel cover the dough ball until using.
7. Drain the potatoes well and mash them into a bowl.
8. In another small bowl, add the mustard seeds, cumin, curry powder, ground ginger and red pepper flakes and mix well.
9. In a pan, add 1 1/2 tsp of the oil over medium heat and cook until heated through.
10. Add the carrot, garlic and onion and stir fry for about 5 minutes.
11. Add the spice mixture and stir fry for about 1 minute.

12. Stir in the peas and broth and remove from the heat.
13. In the bowl of the potatoes, place the pea's mixture, sugar, salt and pepper and gently, stir to combine.
14. In the bottom of a 9-inch pie dish, place the potato mixture evenly.
15. Dust a smooth surface with the flour lightly.
16. Place the dough onto the surface and with a lightly floured roll pin, roll into an 11-inch circle.
17. Arrange the rolled dough over the potato mixture evenly.
18. With your fingers, press the top of dough t many places to remove air pockets.
19. Then, press the edges to seal the filling and carefully, remove the excess dough.
20. With a knife, make an X shape cut in the middle of dough.
21. Coat the top of dough with milk evenly.
22. Cook in the oven for about 40-50 minutes.
23. Remove from the oven and place the pie dish onto a wire rack for about 5 minutes.
24. Remove the pie from dish and cut into desired sized slices.
25. Serve warm.

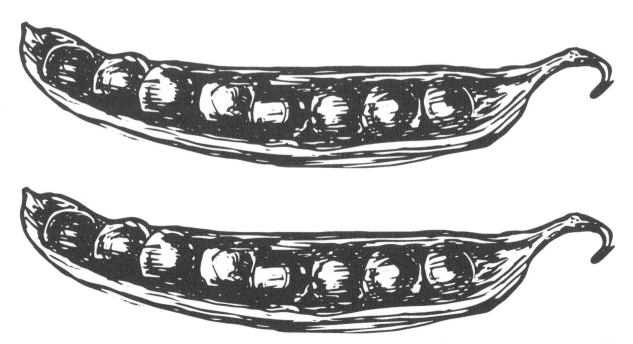

PUNJABI
Grilled Chicken

🥣 Prep Time: 15 mins
🕐 Total Time: 9 hr

Servings per Recipe: 6
Calories	368
Fat	19.5
Carbohydrates	102
Protein	1165
Cholesterol	10.5
Sodium	36.1

Ingredients
3 lb. bone-in chicken pieces
3 tbsp fresh lemon juice
1 tbsp meat tenderizer
2 C. plain yogurt, divided
3 tbsp ground cumin
2 tbsp ground coriander
1/3 C. chopped fresh cilantro
2 tsp paprika

1/2 tsp ground turmeric
2 tsp salt
1 tsp ground black pepper
6 cloves garlic, minced

Directions
1. Use a sharp knife to create deep cuts in each chicken piece.
2. In a small bowl, add the meat tenderizer and lemon juice and stir to combine.
3. Coat the chicken pieces withe lemon mixture evenly.
4. In a food processor, add 1/2 C. yogurt, garlic, cilantro, coriander, cumin, turmeric, paprika, salt and pepper and pulse until pureed finely.
5. In a bowl, add the pureed mixture and remaining yogurt and mix well.
6. In a large bowl, add the chicken and yogurt mixture and mix well.
7. Place the chicken in fridge for the whole night.
8. Set your grill for medium heat and lightly, grease the grill grate.
9. Remove the bowl from the fridge.
10. Place the chicken onto the grill and cook for about 30-45 minutes, flipping occasionally.

Mumbai
Pilaf

Prep Time: 10 mins
Total Time: 50 min

Servings per Recipe: 2
Calories	515
Fat	15.4
Carbohydrates	0
Protein	905
Cholesterol	87.1
Sodium	9.9

Ingredients
2 tbsp vegetable oil
1 onion, thinly sliced
1/2 tsp ground cumin
1 C. Basmati rice, rinsed
2 C. water

3/4 tsp salt
1/2 tsp garam masala
3/4 C. frozen mixed vegetables

Directions
1. Add oil in a pot over medium heat and cook until heated through.
2. Add the cumin and onion and stir fry for about 3-4 minutes.
3. Add the rice, vegetables, garam masala, salt and water and mix well.
4. Set the heat to high and cook until boiling.
5. Cover the pan and Set the heat to low.
6. Cook for about 10 minutes, without stirring.
7. Now, mix the rice mixture and cook for about 25-30 minutes.
8. Serve hot.

COUSCOUS
Curried

Prep Time: 10 mins
Total Time: 30 mins

Servings per Recipe: 3
Calories	413
Fat	18
Carbohydrates	0
Protein	317
Cholesterol	45.6
Sodium	22

Ingredients

1 C. vegetable broth
1/2 C. couscous
1 tbsp canola oil
1 tsp ajwain (carom) seeds
1 clove garlic, coarsely chopped
1 tsp turmeric powder
1 tsp curry powder
1/2 tsp asafoetida powder (hing)
1 pinch chili powder

1 pinch ground cinnamon
1 (12 oz.) package frozen shelled edamame (green soybeans)
1 bunch broccoli, cut into florets
sea salt to taste
ground black pepper to taste
1 tbsp toasted sesame oil

Directions

1. In a pot, add the broth over high heat and cook until boiling.
2. Set the heat to medium and stir in the couscous.
3. Cook for 10 minutes.
4. Remove from the heat and with a fork, fluff the couscous.
5. In another pan, add the oil over medium-high heat and cook until heated completely.
6. Add the ajwain seeds and stir fry for about 30 seconds.
7. Set the heat to medium.
8. Add the garlic, curry powder, cinnamon, hing powder, chili powder and turmeric and stir fry for about 3 minutes.
9. Add the broccol, edamame, salt and black pepper and cook for about 5 minutes.
10. Remove from the heat and drizzle the veggie mixture with the sesame oil.
11. Serve the couscous with a topping of the veggie mixture.

Eggplant
Gujarati

 Prep Time: 10 mins

⏱ Total Time: 40 min

Servings per Recipe: 4
Calories	533
Fat	39.7
Carbohydrates	87
Protein	839
Cholesterol	44.5
Sodium	7.1

Ingredients

2 1/2 lb. eggplant, halved
2/3 C. clarified butter
1 C. chopped onions
4 large ripe tomatoes, chopped
4 tsp crushed coriander seed

Directions

1. Set your oven to 325 degrees F before doing anything else and lightly, grease a baking sheet.
2. Arrange the eggplant halves onto the prepared baking sheet and cook in the oven for about 20 minutes.
3. Remove from the oven and with a potato masher, mash the eggplant.
4. In a frying pan, add the clarified butter over medium heat and cook until melted.
5. Add the onion and cook for about 4-5 minutes.
6. Add the eggplant and tomatoes and cook until all the liquid is absorbed, mixing frequently.
7. Serve with a garnishing of the coriander.

RAJ'S
Chapati

Prep Time: 15 mins
Total Time: 30 mins

Servings per Recipe: 10
Calories	110
Fat	3
Carbohydrates	0
Protein	234
Cholesterol	18.2
Sodium	2.9

Ingredients
1 C. whole wheat flour
1 C. all-purpose flour
1 tsp salt
2 tbsp olive oil
3/4 C. hot water

Directions
1. Add the flours and salt in a bowl and mix well.
2. Add the required amount of the water and oil and mix until an elastic and non-sticky dough is formed.
3. Place the dough onto a floured surface and with your hands, knead until a smooth dough is formed.
4. Make about 10 balls from the dough and keep aside for some time.
5. Place 1 dough ball onto a floured surface and roll into a thin tortilla.
6. Grease a large frying pan and heat over medium heat.
7. Cook the tortilla until cooked from both sides.
8. Repeat with the remaining dough balls.

Kerala Tofu Curry

Prep Time: 25 mins
Total Time: 45 mins

Servings per Recipe: 4
Calories	323
Fat	21.6
Carbohydrates	0
Protein	175
Cholesterol	19.1
Sodium	17.7

Ingredients

1 tbsp sesame oil
5 cloves garlic, minced
1 tbsp minced ginger
1 firm mango, peeled and sliced
3 tbsp yellow curry powder
2 tbsp chopped cilantro

1 can light coconut milk
1 package extra firm tofu, cubed
1/4 tsp salt and pepper

Directions

1. In a skillet, add the oil over medium-high heat and cook until heated through.
2. Add the ginger and garlic and stir fry for about 1 minute.
3. Stir in the mango and and stir fry for about 1 minute.
4. Add the cilantro and curry powder and stir fry for about 1 minute.
5. Add the coconut milk and cook until just boiling, stirring occasionally.
6. Add the tofu, salt and black pepper and cook for about 5 minutes, mixing as required.

KERALA SEAFOOD
Curry

Prep Time: 30 mins
Total Time: 1 hr 25 mins

Servings per Recipe: 4
Calories	338
Fat	13.5
Carbohydrates	56
Protein	2715
Cholesterol	11.6
Sodium	41.6

Ingredients
2 tsp Dijon mustard
1 tsp ground black pepper
1/2 tsp salt
2 tbsp canola oil
4 white fish fillets
1 onion, coarsely chopped
4 cloves garlic, roughly chopped
1 piece fresh ginger root, chopped
5 cashew halves
1 tbsp canola oil
2 tsp cayenne pepper

1/2 tsp ground turmeric
1 tsp ground cumin
1 tsp ground coriander
1 tsp salt
1 tsp white sugar
1/2 C. chopped tomato
1/4 C. vegetable broth
1/4 C. chopped fresh cilantro

Directions
1. In a shallow dish, add 2 tbsp of canola oil, mustard, 1/2 tsp of the salt and black pepper and mix until well combined.
2. In the bowl, place the fish fillets and mix well with the oil mixture.
3. Place in the fridge for about 30 - 40 minutes.
4. Set your oven to 350 degrees F.
5. In a food processor, add the cashews, onion, ginger and garlic and process until smooth.
6. In a pan, add 1 tbsp of the canola oil over medium - low heat and cook until heated through.
7. Add the cashew puree and stir fry for about 2 minutes.
8. Stir in the sugar, coriander, cumin, turmeric, cayenne pepper and 1 tsp of the salt and stir fry for about 5 minutes.
9. Add the broth and tomato and stir to combine well.
10. Remove the fish fillets from the bowl and shake off to remove excess marinade.

11. In the bottom of a baking dish, place the fish fillets in a single layer.

12. Place the tomato mixture over the fish fillets over the fillets evenly.

13. Cover the baking dish with a lid and cook in the oven for about 30 minutes.

14. Serve with a garnishing of the cilantro.

HOW TO MAKE
Traditional Flat Bread (Naan)

Prep Time: 25 mins
Total Time: 2 hr 25 mins

Servings per Recipe: 6
Calories   237
Fat   9.3
Carbohydrates   23
Protein   393
Cholesterol   33.3
Sodium   4.9

Ingredients
2/3 C. warm water
1 tsp active dry yeast
1 tsp white sugar
2 C. all-purpose flour
1 tsp salt

1/4 C. ghee
2 tbsp plain yogurt
2 tsp kalonji (onion seed)

Directions
1. In a bowl, add the sugar, yeast and warm water and stir until well combined.
2. With a lid, cover the bowl and keep aside in a warm place for about 8-10 minutes.
3. In a bowl, sift together the salt and flour for at least 3 times.
4. Add the yogurt, half of the ghee and yeast mixture and mix until a dough holds together.
5. Place the dough onto a generously floured smooth surface and with your hands, knead until an elastic dough is formed.
6. In an oiled bowl, place the dough and turn to coat with the oil.
7. With a plastic wrap, cover the bowl keep aside in a warm place for about 1 1/2 hours.
8. Set the broiler of your oven and line a baking sheet with a greased piece of foil.
9. Remove the plastic warp and with your hands, punch down the dough for a while.
10. Now, again with your hands, knead the dough for at least 5 minutes.
11. Make about 6 equal sized balls from the dough.
12. Place 1 ball onto a floured surface and with a rolling pain, roll into an 8-inch circle.
13. Coat the naan with the ghee slightly and top with a little kalonji.
14. Arrange the naan onto the prepared baking sheet ad cook under the broiler for 2 minutes per side.
15. Repeat with the remaining dough balls.

Indian
Potato and Peas Pot

🥣 Prep Time: 20 mins
🕐 Total Time: 4 hr 20 mins

Servings per Recipe: 8
Calories   370
Fat   18.3
Carbohydrates   0
Protein   373
Cholesterol   48.8
Sodium   8.2

Ingredients

5 russet potatoes, peeled and cut into 1-inch cubes
1/4 C. curry powder
2 tbsp flour
1 tbsp chili powder
1/2 tsp red pepper flakes
1/2 tsp cayenne pepper
1 large green bell pepper, cut into strips

1 large red bell pepper, cut into strips
1 (1 oz.) package dry onion soup mix
1 can unsweetened coconut cream
water, as needed
1 1/2 C. matchstick-cut carrots
1 C. green peas
1/4 C. chopped fresh cilantro

Directions

1. In a slow cooker, add the potatoes, bell peppers, coconut cream, flour, curry powder, chili powder, cayenne pepper and red pepper flakes and mix until well blended.
2. Set the slow cooker on Low and cook, covered for about 3-4 hours.
3. Uncover and stir in the carrots.
4. Cook, covered for about 1/2 hour.
5. Uncover and stir in the peas.
6. Cook, covered for about 1/2 hour more.
7. Serve hot with a garnishing of the cilantro.

SIMPLE
Curried Potatoes

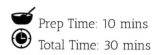

Prep Time: 10 mins
Total Time: 30 mins

Servings per Recipe: 5
Calories	268
Fat	4.7
Carbohydrates	0
Protein	267
Cholesterol	52.1
Sodium	6.3

Ingredients
1 C. vegetable oil for frying
2 cloves garlic, pressed
1 tsp cumin seeds
1/2 tsp salt
1/4 tsp turmeric

1/4 tsp black pepper
5 russet potatoes, cubed
2 tbsp fresh cilantro
1 tsp curry paste

Directions
1. In a skillet, mix together the oil, garlic, turmeric, cumin, salt and black pepper over medium heat and cook until heated completely.
2. Add the potatoes and cook for about 12-15 minutes, flipping as required.
3. Stir in the curry paste and cilantro and cook for 1 more minute.
4. Serve hot.

Pot Roast
Gwalior

Prep Time: 30 mins
Total Time: 6 hr

Servings per Recipe: 12
Calories   271
Fat   18.4
Carbohydrates   69
Protein   172
Cholesterol   7.6
Sodium   18.7

Ingredients

4 lb boneless beef chuck roast
3 cloves garlic, crushed
1 piece ginger, crushed
3 dried red chilies, broken
3 whole black peppercorns, crushed
3 whole cloves
1 piece cinnamon stick
1/2 tsp cumin seeds
1/2 tsp ground coriander
salt to taste

3 C. water
1 tbsp vegetable oil
2 onions, sliced
1/2 tsp chili powder
2 large tomatoes, chopped
1/2 C. ketchup
2 tbsp tomato puree
1 tsp ground black pepper
2 tbsp chopped fresh cilantro

Directions

1. In the bottom of a slow cooker, mix together the roast, chilies, ginger, garlic, spices, salt and water.
2. Set the slow cooker on High and cook, covered for about 4-6 hours.
3. Uncover the slow cooker and transfer the roast onto a cutting board to cool slightly.
4. With a sharp knife, cut the roast into thick slices.
5. Through a fine mesh strainer, strain the cooking liquid into a bowl and discard the solids.
6. Set your oven to 350 degrees F.
7. In an oven-proof pan, add the oil over medium heat and cook until heated.
8. Add the onion and stir fry for about 6-7 minutes.
9. Add the chili powder and stir fry for about 30 seconds.
10. Add the strained cooking liquid, tomato puree, ketchup, tomatoes and black pepper and cook for 10 minutes.
11. Stir in the roast slices and cook for about 8-10 minutes.

12. Transfer the pan into the oven and cook for about 10-15 minutes, coating with the pan sauce
13. Serve with a topping of the cilantro.

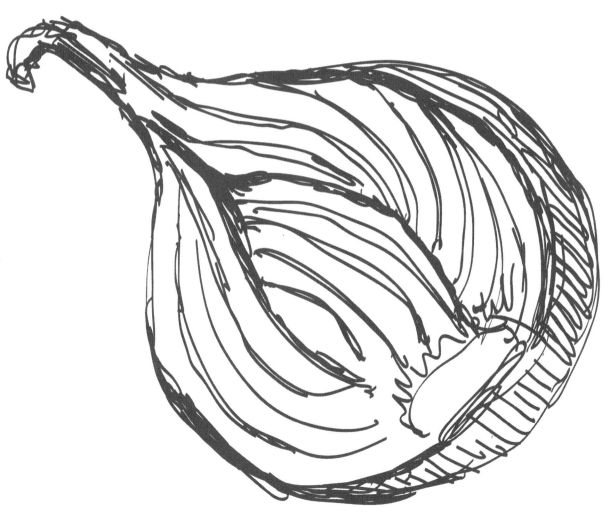

Maharashtra
Broccoli

Prep Time: 15 mins
Total Time: 32 mins

Servings per Recipe: 4
Calories   164
Fat   12.3
Carbohydrates   0
Protein   132.3
Cholesterol   10.2
Sodium   3.5

Ingredients

3 tbsp vegetable oil
1/2 tsp mustard seed
1 small onion, chopped
1/2 tsp cumin seeds
1 tbsp ginger-garlic paste
1 tsp chili powder
1 tsp ground turmeric

1 head broccoli, chopped
2 tsp water
2 tsp salt
3 tbsp garbanzo bean flour
1 tsp vegetable oil

Directions

1. In a pan, add 3 tbsp of the oil over medium heat and cook until heated.
2. Stir in the mustard seeds and stir fry fr about 1 minute.
3. Stir in the onion and cumin seeds and stir fry for about 5-6 minutes.
4. Stir in the turmeric, chili powder, ginger and garlic paste and stir fry for about 1-2 minutes.
5. Stir in the broccoli and cook for about 9-10 minutes.
6. Stir in the salt and water and stir fry for about 1 minute.
7. Slowly, add the gram flour, stirring continuously until well combined.
8. Stir fry for about 6-8 minutes.
9. Serve with a drizzling of some oil.

ANIKA'S DHAL MAKHANI
(Lentil Curry)

Prep Time: 15 mins
Total Time: 4 hr 15 mins

Servings per Recipe: 6
Calories	375
Fat	21.2
Carbohydrates	48
Protein	2718
Cholesterol	34.2
Sodium	12.8

Ingredients

1 C. lentils
1/4 C. dry kidney beans
water to cover
5 C. water
2 tbsp salt
2 tbsp vegetable oil
1 tbsp cumin seeds
4 cardamom pods
1 cinnamon stick, broken
4 bay leaves
6 whole cloves
1 1/2 tbsp ginger paste

1 1/2 tbsp garlic paste
1/2 tsp ground turmeric
1 pinch cayenne pepper
1 C. canned tomato puree
1 tbsp chili powder
2 tbsp ground coriander
1/4 C. butter
2 tbsp dried fenugreek leaves
1/2 C. cream

Directions

1. In a large bowl of the water, soak the kidney beans and lentils for whole night.
2. Drain well and transfer into a pan over medium heat.
3. Add the salt and water and cook for about 1 hour, stirring often.
4. Remove from the heat and keep aside.
5. In a skillet, add the oil over medium-high heat and cook until heated completely.
6. Add the bay leaves, cumin seeds, cinnamon stick, cardamom pods and cloves and stir fry for about about 1 minute.
7. Set the heat to medium-low and stir in the garlic paste, ginger paste, cayenne pepper and turmeric.
8. Add the tomato puree and cook for 5-6 minutes.
9. Stir in the butter, chili powder and coriander until butter melts completely.
10. Add the kidney beans, lentils with the cooking liquid and cook until boiling.

11. Set the heat to low and stir in the fenugreek.
12. Cook, covered for about 45 minutes, mixing as required.
13. Stir in the cream and cook for about 3-4 minutes.

SIMPLE
Coconut Curry

Prep Time: 15 mins
Total Time: 46 mins

Servings per Recipe: 8
Calories   409
Fat   15
Carbohydrates   61
Protein   352
Cholesterol   44.4
Sodium   25.2

Ingredients

8 boneless, skinless chicken breast halves,
cut each in 2 pieces
1 tbsp mild curry powder
3 tsp ground cinnamon
3 whole cloves
1 1/4 tsp minced fresh ginger root

1 tsp finely chopped garlic
olive oil, as needed
2 onions, thinly sliced
1 can cream of coconut
1 can tomato sauce

Directions

1. In a bowl, add the garlic, ginger, curry powder, cloves and cinnamon and mix well.

2. In a pan, add the oil over medium-high heat and cook until heated through.

3. Add the chicken pieces and sear for about 3-4 minutes from both sides.

4. With a slotted spoon, transfer the chicken into a bowl.

5. In the skillet, add the onion and stir fry for about 4-5 minutes.

6. Add the cooked chicken, tomato sauce, cream of coconut and garlic mixture and mix well.

7. Set the heat to low and cook for about 20-25 minutes.

How to Make
Chickpeas

🥣 Prep Time: 25 mins

🕐 Total Time: 45 mins

Servings per Recipe: 6
Calories   232
Fat   6.5
Carbohydrates   0
Protein   542
Cholesterol   36.9
Sodium   7.9

Ingredients

2 tbsp vegetable oil
4 cloves garlic, minced
1/2 C. onion, chopped
1 tbsp minced fresh ginger root
1/8 tsp garam masala
2 tsp channa masala spice mix

1 large tomato, chopped
1 1/2 C. water
2 cans garbanzo beans, drained
salt to taste

Directions

1. In a pot, add the oil over medium-high heat and cook until heated completely.
2. Stir in the onion, ginger and garlic and cook for about 4-5 minutes.
3. Stir in the beans, tomato, garam masala, channa masala spice, salt and water and cook until boiling.
4. Set the heat to low and cook, covered for 20 minutes.

PUNJABI
Greens Curry

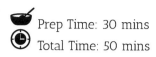 Prep Time: 30 mins
Total Time: 50 mins

Servings per Recipe: 6
Calories	182
Fat	16.2
Carbohydrates	41
Protein	565
Cholesterol	7.6
Sodium	4.7

Ingredients
1/2 C. butter
2 tsp cumin seed
1 green chile pepper, diced
2 cloves garlic, chopped
2 tbsp ground turmeric
1 lb. chopped mustard greens

1 lb. chopped spinach
1 tsp ground cumin
1 tsp ground coriander
1 tsp salt

Directions
1. Add the butter in a large pan over medium-high heat and cook until melted.
2. Add the garlic, chile pepper, turmeric and cumin seeds and stir fry for about 2 minutes.
3. Add the spinach and mustard greens and stir to combine.
4. Stir fry until the greens are wilted completely.
5. Add the salt, coriander and cumin and stir to combine.
6. Set the heat to low and cook, covered for 8-10 minutes.

South Indian
Veggie Salad

Prep Time: 30 mins
Total Time: 1 hr

Servings per Recipe: 4
Calories   221
Fat   1.6
Carbohydrates   0
Protein   456
Cholesterol   47.7
Sodium   6.7

Ingredients

1 (16 oz.) can garbanzo beans (chickpeas), rinsed and drained
1 mango - peeled and diced
1 C. chopped hearts of romaine
1/2 C. diced cucumber
1/2 C. diced carrot

1/4 C. diced celery
2 tbsp fresh lemon juice
salt to taste
1 C. chopped pineapple

Directions

1. In a serving bowl, add all the ingredients except the pineapple and gently, toss to coat well.

2. Keep aside for about 35-40 minutes before serving.

3. Serve with a garnishing of the pineapple pieces.

NORTH INDIAN
Onion Dip

Prep Time: 10 mins
Total Time: 2 hr 10 mins

Servings per Recipe: 10
Calories   11
Fat   0.1
Carbohydrates   0
Protein   123
Cholesterol   2.7
Sodium   0.3

Ingredients
1 onion, chopped
1 1/2 tbsp lemon juice
1 tsp ketchup
1/2 tsp cayenne pepper

1/2 tsp Hungarian paprika
1/2 tsp salt
1 pinch white sugar

Directions
1. In a food processor, add the onion and process until minced.
2. Add the remaining ingredients and process until smooth.
3. Place into jar and place i the fridge for about 3-4 hours before serving.

Cashew
Pilaf

🥣 Prep Time: 15 mins

🕐 Total Time: 40 mins

Servings per Recipe: 6
Calories	349
Fat	8.6
Carbohydrates	2
Protein	265
Cholesterol	59.5
Sodium	8.2

Ingredients

4 C. water
2 C. long grain rice, rinsed and drained
1/2 tsp salt
2 tbsp vegetable oil, divided
1/4 C. coarsely chopped cashews
7 small dried chile peppers
1 tsp mustard seed

1 tsp cumin seed
10 fresh curry leaves
1 tsp ground turmeric
1/4 C. fresh lime juice
2 tbsp tamarind paste
1 C. plain yogurt

Directions

1. In a pot, add the water and cook until boiling.
2. Add the salt and rice and stir to combine.
3. Set the heat to low and with a id cover the pan.
4. Cook for about 20 - 22 minutes.
5. Meanwhile, in a frying pan, add 1/2 tbsp of the oil over medium heat and cook until heated.
6. Stir in the cashews and cook for 5 minutes.
7. Transfer the cashews into a bowl and keep aside.
8. In the frying pan, add the remaining oil over medium heat and cook until heated.
9. Stir in the cumin seeds, mustard seeds and chile peppers and stir fry for about 30 seconds.
10. Stir in 1/2 of the cashews and curry leaves and stir fry for about 3 minutes.
11. Remove the rice from the heat and stir in the tamarind paste, lime juice and turmeric.
12. Now, place onto a platter and stir in the oil mixture.
13. Serve with a garnishing of the remaining cashews.

CURRIED
Eggs for Breakfast

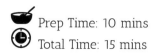

Prep Time: 10 mins
Total Time: 15 mins

Servings per Recipe: 2
Calories	377
Fat	35.5
Carbohydrates	286
Protein	203
Cholesterol	4
Sodium	12.3

Ingredients
1 tsp oil
2 medium eggs
1/2 C. heavy whipping cream
1/4 clove garlic, minced

1/4 C. shredded Cheddar cheese
2 tsp curry powder
1 tsp ground cumin

Directions
1. In a bowl, add the cream and eggs and beat until well combined.
2. Add the remaining ingredients except the oil and mix well.
3. In a frying pan, add the oil over medium-high heat and cook until heated trough.
4. add he egg mixture and cook for about 4-5 minutes, stirring continuously.
5. Serve hot.

Roghan Ghosht (Kashmiri Lamb Curry)

🥣 Prep Time: 30 mins
🕐 Total Time: 2 hr 30 mins

Servings per Recipe: 4

Calories	1041.4
Fat	89.2g
Cholesterol	182.9mg
Sodium	756.0mg
Carbohydrates	15.7g
Protein	44.4g

Ingredients

2 1/2 cm fresh ginger, chopped
8 garlic cloves, peeled
4 tbsp water
275 ml water
10 tbsp vegetable oil
1 kg boneless lamb shoulder
10 whole cardamom pods
2 bay leaves
6 whole cloves
10 whole peppercorns
2 1/2 cm cinnamon sticks

4 medium onions, chopped
1 tsp ground coriander
2 tsp cumin seeds
4 tsp paprika
1 tsp cayenne pepper
1 tsp salt
6 tbsp plain yogurt
1/4 tsp garam masala
ground pepper

Directions

1. In a blender, add 4 tbsp of the water, garlic and ginger and pulse until smooth.
2. In a pan, add the oil and cook until melted.
3. Add the lamb pieces in batches and cook until browned completely.
4. With a slotted spoon transfer the lamb pieces into a bowl.
5. In the pan, add the bay leaves, cinnamon, cardamom, cloves and peppercorns and stir fry for about 1 minute.
6. Add the onions and sauté for 5 minutes.
7. Add the garlic puree mixture and sauté for 30 seconds.
8. Add the cumin, coriander, cayenne, paprika and salt and sauté for about 30 seconds.
9. Stir in the cooked lab pieces and sauté for about 1 minute.
10. Slowly, add the yoghurt and cook for about 2-3 minutes, stirring frequently.

11. Add the remaining water and cook until boiling, stirring continuously.

12. Set the heat to low and simmer, covered for about 1-1 1/2 hours, stirring occasionally.

13. Now, set the heat to medium and cook for about 4-5 minutes.

14. Stir in the garam masala and black pepper and serve.

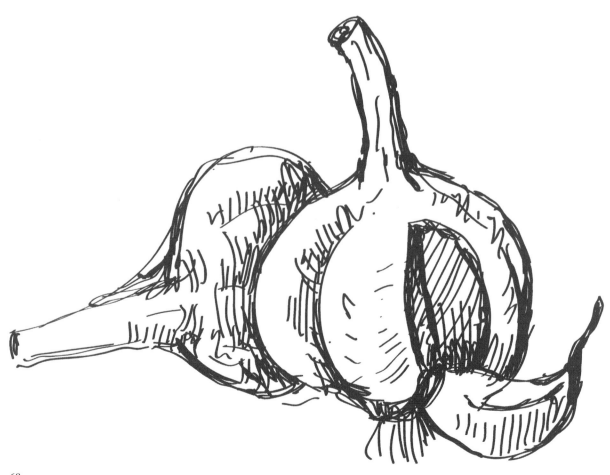

Palak
(Spicy Spinach)

Prep Time: 10 mins
Total Time: 30 mins

Servings per Recipe: 2
Calories	404.3
Fat	26.8g
Cholesterol	65.5mg
Sodium	134.7mg
Carbohydrates	37.9g
Protein	8.6g

Ingredients
300 g spinach, frozen
2 garlic cloves, chopped
1 inch fresh ginger, chopped
2 onions, chopped
1-2 green chili, chopped
200 g potatoes, cubed
1 tsp turmeric
4 tbsp ghee

1 tsp cumin seed
1 tsp garam masala
1/2 tsp ground coriander
1/2 tsp ground cumin
1 tbsp fresh cream
salt

Directions
1. Add the spinach, onion, ginger and garlic in a skillet and cook for 8-10 minutes.
2. Remove from the heat and keep aside o cool slightly.
3. In a blender, add the spinach mixture and pulse until smooth.
4. In a pan of the salted boiling water, cook the potatoes and turmeric for about 10 minutes.
5. Drain the potatoes and keep aside.
6. In a skillet, add the ghee and cook until melted.
7. Add the spinach puree and cumin and cook for about 2-3 minutes.
8. Stir in the spices and boiled potatoes and cook for about 2-3 minutes.
9. Stir in the cream and serve.

PRIYANKA'S DHAL
(Lentil Curry)

Prep Time: 30 mins
Total Time: 1 hr 5 mins

Servings per Recipe: 6

Calories	93.1
Fat	0.3g
Cholesterol	0.0mg
Sodium	6.1mg
Carbohydrates	16.9g
Protein	6.6g

Ingredients

2 C. lentils, cooked
1 large yellow onion, chopped
1 bunch cilantro, chopped
1 large tomatoes
1 can coconut milk
1 can tomato sauce
curry powder

turmeric
ginger
ground cloves
cumin
cayenne
salt

Directions

1. In a pan, heat the oil and sauté the onion for about 4-5 minutes.

2. Stir in the cilantro and sauté for about 3-5 minutes more.

3. Stir in the tomato and cook for about 2-3 minutes.

4. Stir in the coconut milk, tomato sauce, ginger, curry powder, turmeric, cloves, cumin, cayenne and salt and cook for 1/2 hour.

Punjabi
Chickpeas I

🍲 Prep Time: 5 mins
🕐 Total Time: 35 mins

Servings per Recipe: 4
Calories   300.0
Fat   2.9g
Cholesterol   0.0mg
Sodium   643.6mg
Carbohydrates   58.3g
Protein   12.2g

Ingredients

2 medium onions, chopped
1 tbsp grated ginger
2 tbsp chopped garlic
1 1/2 tsp cumin seeds
1 bay leaf
1/2 inch cinnamon stick
2 tomatoes, chopped
1 tsp ground coriander

1/2 tsp turmeric
salt
1/4-1/2 tsp cayenne pepper
2 cans garbanzo beans
1/2-1 tsp garam masala
1 tbsp fresh lemon juice

Directions

1. Heat a skillet and stir fry the bay leaf, cinnamon stick and cumin seeds for about 30 seconds.
2. Stir in the garlic and ginger and stir fry for about 1 minute.
3. Stir in the onion and stir fry for about 3-4 minutes, adding a little water occasionally.
4. Stir in the tomatoes, turmeric, coriander, cayenne pepper and salt, and cook until boiling.
5. Stir in the chickpeas and set the heat to low.
6. cook, covered for about 12-15 minutes.
7. Remove from the heat and stir in the lemon juice and garam masala.

FRIED
Bread Skillet

Prep Time: 10 mins
Total Time: 13 mins

Servings per Recipe: 8
Calories   167.4
Fat   2.0g
Cholesterol   4.2mg
Sodium   206.4mg
Carbohydrates   31.5g
Protein   5.0g

Ingredients
vegetable oil
2 1/2 C. flour
1/2 tsp salt
1 tsp baking powder
1/4 tsp sugar
1 tsp oil
1 C. warm milk

Directions
1. Add all the ingredients except the oil in a bowl and mix until a dough is formed.
2. Divide dough into equal sized portions.
3. Roll each dough portion into a circle.
4. In a frying pan, add the oil over medium-high heat and cook until melted.
5. Add the dough circles, one at a time and cook until golden brown from both sides.
6. Serve immediately.

Chai Masala
Tea at Home

Prep Time: 5 mins
Total Time: 15 mins

Servings per Recipe: 3
Calories	116.5
Fat	2.9g
Cholesterol	11.3mg
Sodium	44.7mg
Carbohydrates	20.4g
Protein	2.6g

Ingredients

2 C. water
3-5 cloves
1 cinnamon stick, crushed
2-3 cardamom pods, crushed
1/4 C. sugar
1 C. milk
2 tbsp black tea leaves

Directions

1. In a pan, add the cloves, cinnamon stick and cardamom pods and water and cook until boiling.
2. set the heat to low and cook, covered for about 2-3 minutes.
3. Stir in the milk and sugar and cook until boiling stirring frequently.
4. Stir in the tea leaves and immediately, cover the pan.
5. Remove from the heat and keep aide, covered for about 5 minutes.
6. Through a strainer, strain he tea into cups and serve.

KOTA
Pudding

Prep Time: 5 mins
Total Time: 30 mins

Servings per Recipe: 4
Calories	423.4
Fat	27.0g
Cholesterol	46.8mg
Sodium	45.0mg
Carbohydrates	42.1g
Protein	7.0g

Ingredients

1 C. cooked long-grain rice
1 C. whole milk
1/2 C. heavy cream
3/4 C. coconut milk
2 oz. sugar

1/4 tsp ground cardamom
1 1/2 oz. golden raisins
1 1/2 oz. chopped unsalted pistachios

Directions

1. Add the whole milk and rice in a pan and cook over medium heat until boiling.
2. Set the heat to low and simmer for about 4-5 minutes, mixing as required.
3. Now, set the heat to medium and stir in the sugar, coconut milk, heavy cream and cardamom.
4. Cook for about 8-10 minutes, beating frequently.
5. Remove the pan from the heat.
6. immediately, add the pistachios and raisins and stir to combine.
7. In a serving bowl, place the pudding and with a plastic warp, cover the pudding surface.
8. Refrigerate to chill before serving.

Kerala
Pumpkin Stew

🥣 Prep Time:1 hr
🕐 Total Time: 3 hr

Servings per Recipe: 1
Calories	245.2
Fat	13.6g
Cholesterol	18.5mg
Sodium	490.1mg
Carbohydrates	25.4g
Protein	7.9g

Ingredients

2 lb. cooking pumpkin, chunked
1 lb sweet potato, chunked
2 tbsp melted butter
1 tbsp brown sugar
1 tsp salt
1 tsp black pepper
2 tbsp oil
1 large Spanish onion, chopped
1 scotch bonnet peppers, chopped
1 tbsp minced garlic
1 tbsp fresh ginger, grated
2 tbsp fresh thyme

2 tsp orange zest
1 tbsp curry powder
1/4 tsp ground allspice
1 cinnamon stick
2 bay leaves
6 C. chicken stock
1/4 C. heavy cream
1/4 C. unsweetened coconut milk
1/2 C. toasted pumpkin seeds

Directions

1. Set your oven to 350 degrees F before doing anything else and grease a large roasting pan.
2. Add the sweet potatoes, pumpkin, brown sugar, butter, salt and black pepper and mix well.
3. In the bottom of the prepared roasting pan, arrange the vegetable mixture in a single layer.
4. Cook in the oven for about 1-1 1/2 hours.
5. Remove from the oven and keep aside.
6. In a large soup pot, heat the oil and stir fry the onion for about 4-6 minutes.
7. Add the ginger, garlic and scotch bonnet and stir fry for about 1 minute.
8. Add the orange peel, thyme, curry powder, bay leaves, cinnamon stick and allspice and stir

until well combined.

9. Stir in the roasted veggies and chicken stock and cook until boiling.

10. Set the heat to low and cook, covered for about 30 minutes, mixing time by time.

11. Remove from the heat and keep aside to cool slightly.

12. In a blender, add the soup mixture in batches and pulse until pureed finely.

13. In the same pan, add the pureed soup, coconut milk and cream and cook until heated completely, stirring frequently

14. Serve hot with a topping of the pumpkin seeds.

Potatoes
Tandoori

Prep Time: 15 mins
Total Time: 1 hr

Servings per Recipe: 4

Calories	98.6
Fat	4.5g
Cholesterol	0.0mg
Sodium	544.7mg
Carbohydrates	13.6g
Protein	1.4g

Ingredients
2 sweet potatoes, cubed
1 tbsp tandoori paste
1 tbsp olive oil
1 tbsp sesame seeds
1/2 tsp salt

1/2 tsp red pepper flakes
cooking spray
1/2 tsp kosher salt

Directions
1. Set your oven to 375 degrees F before doing anything else and line a baking sheet with a piece of foil. Arrange a rack in the bottom shelf of oven.
2. In a bowl, place the sweet potato cubes, sesame seeds, tandoori paste, oil, red pepper flakes and 1/2 tsp of the salt and toss to coat well.
3. In the bottom of the prepared baking sheet, arrange the sweet potato cubes in a single layer.
4. Cook in the oven for about 35-40 minutes, flipping once after 20 minutes.
5. Serve with a sprinkling of the remaining salt.

INDIAN
Fried Onions (Bhaji)

Prep Time: 5 mins
Total Time: 20 mins

Servings per Recipe: 4
Calories	1691.4
Fat	167.1g
Cholesterol	0.0mg
Sodium	132.7mg
Carbohydrates	40.7g
Protein	12.4g

Ingredients

2 large onions, sliced
200 g chickpea flour
1 tsp baking powder
2 tbsp rice flour
1 tsp turmeric
1/2 tsp black onion seeds
1/2 tsp chili powder

1/2 tsp cumin, ground
1/2 tsp coriander, ground
salt
100 ml water
750 ml vegetable oil

Directions

1. Add the flours, baking powder, onion seeds, salt, ground spices and water and stir until well combined.
2. Gently, fold in the onion slices.
3. In a skillet, heat the oil over medium-high heat.
4. With a spoon, place th mixture in skillet in batches and cook for about 1-2 minutes.
5. Transfer the fritters onto a paper towel-lined plate to drain.
6. Serve with a sprinkling of the salt.

Cookies
for Chai

Prep Time: 10 mins

Total Time: 25 mins

Servings per Recipe: 10

Calories	308.3
Fat	17.6g
Cholesterol	18.6mg
Sodium	192.8mg
Carbohydrates	33.7g
Protein	5.4g

Ingredients
1/2 C. oil
3/4 C. brown sugar
1 egg
1/2 tsp vanilla
3/4 C. flour

1/2 tsp baking soda
1/2 tsp salt
1 1/2 C. rolled oats
3/4 C. sunflower seeds

Directions
1. Set your oven to 350 degrees F before doing anything else.
2. In a bowl, mix together the flour, salt and baking soda.
3. In another bowl, add the egg, brown sugar, vanilla and oil and beat until creamy.
4. Add the flour mixture and mix until well combined.
5. Gently, fold in the sunflower seeds and oats.
6. Drop the cookies onto a cookie sheet in a single layer.
7. Cook in the oven for about 10-15 minutes.
8. Remove from the oven and keep onto the wire rack to cool in the pan for about 5 minutes.
9. Carefully, invert the cookies onto the wire rack to cool completely before serving.

Cookies for Chai   79

PUNJABI STYLE
Chickpeas Curry

Prep Time: 10 mins
Total Time: 40 mins

Servings per Recipe: 3
Calories	309.8
Fat	15.9g
Cholesterol	0.0mg
Sodium	1208.4mg
Carbohydrates	35.9g
Protein	8.5g

Ingredients

2 fresh tomatoes, quartered
1/2 inch cube fresh ginger, cut in half
1 fresh green chile
3 tbsp grapeseed oil
1/4 tsp asafoetida powder
1 tsp whole cumin seed
3 C. fresh spinach, chopped
1 cans chickpeas
1/4-1/2 C. water

1 tbsp ground coriander
1/2 tsp ground chili powder
1/2 tsp turmeric
1 tsp sea salt
1/2 tsp garam masala
fresh cilantro, chopped fine

Directions

1. In a blender, add the ginger, green chile and tomatoes and pulse until smooth.
2. Add the oil in a skillet and heat over medium heat.
3. Stir in the cumin seeds and asofetida and stir fry until aromatic.
4. Stir in the tomato puree and stir fry for about 2-3 minutes.
5. Add the chili powder, turmeric, coriander and salt and cook for about 8-10 minutes, stirring frequently.
6. Stir in the spinach and water and cook for about 2-3 minutes.
7. Stir in the chickpeas and garam masala and cook for about 3-4 minutes.
8. Serve with a garnishing of the cilantro.

Indian
Breakfast Omelet

🥣 Prep Time: 10 mins
🕐 Total Time: 20 mins

Servings per Recipe: 1
Calories	495.4
Fat	15.7g
Cholesterol	372.0mg
Sodium	175.0mg
Carbohydrates	95.2g
Protein	19.6g

Ingredients
1 tsp vegetable oil
1 spring onion, minced
1 red onion, chopped
1-2 green chili, chopped
2 cloves garlic, chopped
1/2 inch ginger root, chopped
1/4 tsp turmeric
1 tsp ground cumin

1 tsp ground coriander
2 eggs, beaten
freshly coriander
freshly mint
3-5 drops lime juice
salt

Directions
1. In a non-stick skillet, add the oil and cook until heated completely.
2. Add the garlic, ginger, chili and onion and cook for about 4-5 minutes, stirring frequently.
3. Stir in the cumin, coriander and turmeric and cook for about 1-2 minutes, stirring continuously.
4. Remove from the heat and keep aside.
5. In a large egg, crack the eggs and beat with salt slightly.
6. Add the onion mixture, mint and coriander and stir to combine well.
7. In the same skillet, add the egg mixture and cook until set.
8. Drizzle the omelet with lemon juice and change the side.
9. Cook until set completely.

PUNJABI
Carrot Pudding

Prep Time: 10 mins
Total Time: 1 hr 10 mins

Servings per Recipe: 6
Calories	333.1
Fat	19.4g
Cholesterol	50.1mg
Sodium	246.2mg
Carbohydrates	38.4g
Protein	4.5g

Ingredients
6 medium carrots, shredded
2 C. half-and-half cream
1/2 C. packed brown sugar
1/2 C. golden raisin
1/4 C. butter

1/2 tsp ground cardamom
1/4 tsp salt
1/4 C. unsalted pistachios

Directions
1. In a pot, add the half-and-half and carrots and bring to a boil.
2. Set the heat to low and cook for 45 minutes, stirring as required.
3. Add the butter, raisins, brown sugar, cardamom and salt and stir to combine well.
4. Simmer for about 15 minutes, mixing continuously.
5. Serve warm with a topping of the pistachios.

Curry
Lamb Skillet

🥣 Prep Time: 10 mins
🕐 Total Time: 30 mins

Servings per Recipe: 6
Calories   407.0
Fat   31.4g
Cholesterol   82.9mg
Sodium   486.7mg
Carbohydrates   5.4g
Protein   19.6g

Ingredients

1 1/2 lb. ground lamb
1 large onion, chopped
2 tbsp olive oil
2 tbsp your favorite curry powder
3/4 C. beef broth
4 tsp tomato paste

2 cloves garlic
1 tsp salt
1/8-1/4 tsp red pepper flakes
1/2 tsp ground cumin

Directions

1. Heat a large pan and cook the ground lamb until no more pink.
2. With a slotted spoon, transfer the lamb into a bowl and discard the grease from the pan.
3. Add the oil in the pan and heat it.
4. Add the onion and stir fry for about 4-5 minutes.
5. With a mortar and pastel, make a paste of the garlic and salt.
6. In the pan, add the cooked lamb, tomato paste, curry powder, red pepper flakes, garlic paste and broth and stir to combine.
7. Set the heat to low and cook for about 15-20 minutes
8. Serve hot.

SPINACH
Masala

Prep Time: 30 mins
Total Time: 1 hr

Servings per Recipe: 3
Calories	46.3
Fat	0.9g
Cholesterol	0.0mg
Sodium	673.6mg
Carbohydrates	7.8g
Protein	4.3g

Ingredients
2 garlic cloves
1/2 C. tomato sauce
1 (10 oz.) packages frozen chopped spinach, thawed
1 C. cubed panir (optional)
1 C. low-fat whipping cream
1 tbsp minced ginger

1 tsp garam masala
1 tsp coriander
1 tsp cumin
1 tsp red cayenne pepper
1/2 tsp salt

Directions
1. Grease a skillet with the cooking spray and heat over medium-high heat.
2. Add the ginger and garlic and cook for about 1 minute.
3. Add the garam masala, tomato sauce, cumin, coriander, salt and black pepper and stir to combine well.
4. Set the heat to low and cook, partially covered for about 8-10 minutes, mixing as required.
5. Uncover and slowly, add the spinach, stirring to combine.
6. Cook for about 8-9 minutes, stirring occasionally.
7. Add the cheese and whipping cream and stir until well combined.
8. Cook for abut 3-5 minutes.
9. Remove from the heat and enjoy.

Indian
Square Chicken Thighs

🥣 Prep Time: 10 mins
🕐 Total Time: 40 mins

Servings per Recipe: 8
Calories   271.4
Fat   19.8g
Cholesterol   83.9mg
Sodium   83.7mg
Carbohydrates   5.9g
Protein   17.1g

Ingredients

8 chicken thighs
3 tbsp flour
1 tbsp pepper
2 tbsp oil
1 red onion, chopped
2 cloves garlic, crushed
1/2-1 C. stock

3 tsp curry powder
3 dashes hot pepper sauce
1 lime, zest and juice of
1/4 C. fresh cilantro
1/3 C. sour cream

Directions

1. In a shallow dish, mix together the flour and pepper.
2. Coat the thighs with the flour mixture evenly.
3. In a skillet, heat the oil and sear the chicken thighs until browned completely.
4. With a slotted spoon, transfer the chicken thighs into a bowl.
5. In the same skillet, add garlic, onion and remaining flour mixture and stir fry for about 3-4 minutes.
6. Stir in the red pepper sauce, broth and curry powder and cook for about 2 minutes.
7. Now, cook until boiling.
8. Stir in the cooked chicken, lime juice and lime zest and simmer until desired doneness of chicken.
9. Stir in the sour cream and remove from the heat.
10. Enjoy with a garnishing of the cilantro.

7-INGREDIENT
Chappatis

Prep Time: 1 hr 30 mins
Total Time: 2 hr

Servings per Recipe: 1

Calories	219.3
Fat	4.4g
Cholesterol	1.1mg
Sodium	470.7mg
Carbohydrates	38.5g
Protein	5.4g

Ingredients
6 C. all-purpose flour
2 C. water
1/2 C. milk
1 tbsp salt
1/4 C. oil
melted butter
flour, for rolling out dough

Directions
1. In a large bowl, mix together the flour and salt.
2. Slowly, add water and with your hands, knead until a dough ball is formed.
3. Slowly, add the oil while kneading continuously until well combined.
4. With a clean cloth, cover the dough and keep aside for at least 1 hour.
5. Make 15-20 balls equal sized balls from the dough.
6. Place 1 ball onto a floured surface and roll into a 6-inch circle.
7. Coat the rolled circle with the butter and carefully, fold like a long tube.
8. Fold one end into the center of the tube and press slightly to seam the edge.
9. Fold the other end of the tube over the seam like you fold a letter to obtain a dough bundle
10. Arrange the dough bundles and place onto a well-flour dish.
11. Place 1 roll bundle onto a floured surface and with a rolling pin, roll into a 6-8-inch circle.
12. Place a cast iron frying pan over medium heat and heat it completely.
13. Place one circle and cook for about 30 seconds.
14. Carefully, change the side and brush with the butter.

15. Shuffle the chapatti around the pan rapidly to cook on all sides, flipping over and adding more butter if needed.
16. Transfer the cooked chapatti onto a clean cloth-lined serving dish and cover to keep warm.
17. Repeat with the remaining dough bundles.

AUTHENTIC
Bhindi Masala (Curried Okra)

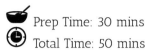

Prep Time: 30 mins
Total Time: 50 mins

Servings per Recipe: 4
Calories	246.9
Fat	21.2g
Cholesterol	0.0mg
Sodium	453.2mg
Carbohydrates	13.9g
Protein	3.0g

Ingredients
1 1/4 tbsp coriander powder
1/4 tsp red chili powder
1/2 tsp turmeric powder
1 medium green chili pepper, chopped
2 medium tomatoes, chopped
1 tbsp cumin seed
1 tsp mustard seeds

1/4 C. oil, to fry ladyfinger
3/4 tsp salt
1/2 lb. okra (bhindi)
2 tbsp oil, for seasoning
2 medium onions, chopped

Directions
1. In a skillet, add the oil over medium heat and cook until heated completely.
2. Add the mustard seeds and seeds and stir fry for about 30 seconds.
3. Stir in the onion and green chili and sauté for about 4-5 minutes,
4. With a slotted spoon, transfer the onion mixture into a bowl.
5. In the same skillet, heat about 1/4 C. of the oil and cook the okra until lightly browned, stirring frequently.
6. Stir in the cooked onion mixture and cook for about 1-2 minutes.
7. Stir in the coriander, turmeric ad chili powder and cook for about 4-5 minutes.
8. Stir in the tomatoes and cook, covered for 6-7 minutes.
9. Stir in the salt and cook, uncovered for about 1-2 minutes.
10. Enjoy hot.

Oriental
Indian Fried Rice

Prep Time: 5 mins
Total Time: 20 mins

Servings per Recipe: 4
Calories   228.5
Fat   3.7g
Cholesterol   93.0mg
Sodium   704.7mg
Carbohydrates   40.7g
Protein   6.6g

Ingredients

1 tsp oil
1 tsp garlic, chopped
2 eggs, whisked
1 C. leftover white rice
2 tbsp fried chicken, diced
2 tbsp spring onions
1 tsp soy sauce

1 tsp salt
1/2 tsp white pepper powder
1/4 tsp sugar
2 tbsp pineapple, chopped
2 tsp raisins
fried cashews

Directions

1. In a skillet, heat the oil and sauté the garlic for about 1-2 minutes.
2. Add the chicken, rice, eggs, spring onion, soy sauce, sugar, salt and white pepper and stir to combine.
3. Stir in the pineapple and raisins and remove from the heat.
4. Enjoy with a garnishing of the cashew.

WEST
Indian Curry

🍲 Prep Time: 20 mins
🕐 Total Time: 1 hr 50 mins

Servings per Recipe: 4
Calories	398.4
Fat	17.9g
Cholesterol	145.1mg
Sodium	210.6mg
Carbohydrates	10.1g
Protein	51.1g

Ingredients

8 cardamom pods, seeds removed
1 tsp fennel seed
8 cloves
4 inches cinnamon sticks
1/2 tsp fenugreek seeds
3/4 tsp black peppercorns
3 tsp coriander seeds
3 tsp cumin seeds
2 - 3 tbsp oil

2 onions, finely chopped
6 garlic cloves, finely minced
4 inches ginger root, grated
2 - 2 1/2 lb. stewing beef, cut in 1 inch cubes
1/2 tsp ground turmeric
2 tsp chili powder
1/2 C. creamed coconut

Directions

1. Place the cardamom seeds, fennel seeds, fenugreek seeds, cumin seeds, coriander seeds, cinnamon stick, cloves and peppercorns in a spice grinder and grind into a fine powder.
2. In a heavy bottomed pan, add the oil and heat over medium heat.
3. Stir in the garlic, ginger and onions and stir fry for about 3-4 minutes.
4. Stir in the beef and sear until no more pink.
5. Stir in the ground spice mixture and stir fry for about 1 minute.
6. Add 1 C. of the water and creamed coconut and mix well.
7. Set the heat to low and simmer, covered for about 1- 1 1/2 hours, mixing occasionally.
8. Stir in the salt and remove from the heat.

Dal
Curry

Prep Time: 20 mins

Total Time: 1 hr 30 mins

Servings per Recipe: 4

Calories	445.0
Fat	15.3g
Cholesterol	30.5mg
Sodium	1362.3mg
Carbohydrates	59.0g
Protein	25.7g

Ingredients

4 tbsp butter
2 medium onions, chopped
1 tsp chili powder
1 1/2 tsp black pepper
2 tsp cumin
1 tsp ground coriander
2 tsp turmeric
1 C. red lentil
1 lemon, juice of

3 C. chicken broth
2 medium broccoli, chopped
1/2 C. dried coconut (optional)
1 tbsp flour
1 tsp salt
1 C. cashews, coarsely chopped (optional)

Directions

1. In a pot, add the butter and cook until melted completely.
2. Add the onion and stir fry for about 4-5 minutes.
3. Stir in the ground spices and stir fry for about and 1-2 minutes.
4. Stir in the lentils, coconut, broth and lemon juice and cook until boiling.
5. Set the heat to low and cook for about 50-55 minutes.
6. Meanwhile, in a steamer, cook the broccoli for about 7 minutes.
7. Remove the broccoli from steamer and immediately, transfer in the bowl of ice water to stop cooking process.
8. With a slotted spoon, transfer about 1/3 C. of the cooking liquid into a bowl with the flour and beat until smooth.
9. In the pot, add the flour mixture, broccoli, cashews and salt and cook for about 4-5 minutes, stirring frequently.
10. Enjoy hot.

RIYA'S
Raita

Prep Time: 35 mins
Total Time: 35 mins

Servings per Recipe: 1
Calories	137.8
Fat	0.5g
Cholesterol	3.6mg
Sodium	152.2mg
Carbohydrates	22.3g
Protein	12.3g

Ingredients

1/2 cucumber, thinly sliced (plus a few
thin slices for garnish)
1 1/2 C. plain nonfat yogurt
6 green onions, thinly sliced
1 - 3 fresh green chili, seeded and finely
chopped
2 tbsp finely chopped fresh cilantro (to
garnish)
salt

Directions

1. Arrange a strainer in the sink.

2. In the strainer, place the cucumber slices and salt and mix well.

3. Let it drain for at least 30 minutes.

4. Squeeze the excess moisture from cucumber slices and then, with paper towels pat dry completely.

5. In a bowl, add the yogurt, cucumber, chilies, green onions and salt and stir to combine well.

6. Garnish the raita with thin cucumber slices and cilantro

7. Enjoy.

Muffins
Kolkata

Prep Time: 10 mins
Total Time: 35 mins

Servings per Recipe: 6
Calories	379.9
Fat	20.0g
Cholesterol	33.8mg
Sodium	342.7mg
Carbohydrates	45.3g
Protein	5.9g

Ingredients

1 egg, beaten
1/2 C. milk
1/4 C. oil
1 tsp vanilla essence
1/2 tsp salt
2 tsp baking powder

1/2 C. sugar
1 C. coconut, grated
1 1/2 C. all-purpose flour (maida)

Directions

1. Set your oven to 350 degrees F before doing anything else and grease a muffin pan.
2. In a bowl. crack the egg and beat slightly.
3. Add the oil, milk and vanilla essence and beat until well combined.
4. Add the flour, coconut, sugar, baking powder and salt and mix until just combined.
5. Transfer the mixture into the prepared muffin cups evenly.
6. Cook in the oven for about 25 minutes or until a toothpick inserted in the center comes out clean.
7. Remove from the oven and keep onto the wire rack to cool in the pan for about 5-10 minutes.
8. Carefully, invert the muffins onto the wire rack to cool completely.
9. Enjoy.

BEEF
Masala

Prep Time: 15 mins
Total Time: 55 mins

Servings per Recipe: 8	
Calories	162.4
Fat	8.1g
Cholesterol	0.9mg
Sodium	396.9mg
Carbohydrates	20.7g
Protein	4.5g

Ingredients

2 kg good quality lean rump steak, cut into cubes
sea salt & freshly ground black pepper
4 tsp garam masala
4 tbsp natural yoghurt
4 - 5 tbsp light olive oil
4 large sweet onions, peeled and finely chopped
4 garlic cloves, peeled and grated
5 cm knob fresh ginger root, peeled and grated
4 tbsp tomato puree
2 tbsp caster sugar
2 (400 g) cans chopped tomatoes

800 ml beef stock
Spice Mix:
handful coriander, leaves separated, stalks finely chopped
6 - 8 cardamom pods
15 - 20 curry leaves
6 long chilies, finely chopped
4 tsp cumin seeds
4 tsp coriander seeds
1 tsp fennel seed
1 tsp fenugreek seeds
4 tsp mild curry powder

Directions

1. In a bowl, add the beef, yoghurt, some olive oil, garam masala, salt and black pepper and mix until well combined. Place in the fridge overnight.
2. Heat a dry non-stick frying pan and cook the fenugreek, fennel, coriander and cumin seeds over high heat for about 1-2 minutes, stirring continuously.
3. Remove from the heat.
4. With a mortar and pestle, grind the toasted spices with a pinch of salt into a fine powder.
5. Add the curry powder and stir to combine well.
6. In a heavy-bottomed pan, add some oil and cook until heated completely.
7. Add the garlic, onions, ginger, chili, coriander stalks, sugar, cardamom pods, ground spice mixture, salt and black pepper and cook for bout 6-8 minutes, stirring occasionally.
8. Meanwhile, heat a skillet and stir fry the beef until browned completely.

9. Remove from the heat and transfer the beef into the pan of the onion mixture.
10. Add the tomato puree and tomatoes over a medium-high heat and cook for about 2-3 minutes.
11. Add the the curry leaves and beef stock and stir o combine.
12. Set the heat to low and cook, covered for about 30 minutes, mixing s required.
13. Enjoy with a garnishing of the coriander leaves.

PUNJABI
Chickpeas II (Chana Masala)

Prep Time: 10 mins
Total Time: 20 mins

Servings per Recipe: 4
Calories	244.9
Fat	11.6g
Cholesterol	0.0mg
Sodium	333.5mg
Carbohydrates	30.4g
Protein	6.4g

Ingredients

1 (15 oz.) cans chickpeas
1 onion, chopped
1 tomatoes, chopped
1 green chili pepper, chopped
4 -5 garlic cloves, chopped
1 inch ginger root, chopped
2 -3 bay leaves

1 tsp red chili powder
1/2 tsp turmeric powder
1 tsp coriander powder
1 tsp garam masala powder
3 tbsp olive oil
coriander leaves, for garnishing

Directions

1. In a food processor, add the tomato, onion, garlic, ginger and green chili and pulse until smooth.
2. In a pan, add the oil over medium heat and cook until heated completely.
3. Add the bay leaves and stir fry for about 30 seconds.
4. Add the pureed mixture and stir fry for about 2-3 minutes.
5. Stir in the garam masala, coriander powder, turmeric, red chili powder and salt and stir fry for 2-3 minutes.
6. Add required amount of water and cook until boiling.
7. Stir in the chickpeas and cook for about 5-7 minutes.
8. Enjoy with a garnishing of the coriander leaves.

Maharashtra
Rice Bowls

🥣 Prep Time: 10 mins
🕐 Total Time: 30 mins

Servings per Recipe: 6
Calories	199.0
Fat	6.8g
Cholesterol	5.0mg
Sodium	109.5mg
Carbohydrates	29.9g
Protein	4.8g

Ingredients

1 C. long-grain rice
2 C. water
1/4 C. roasted peanuts
1 tbsp butter
1 onion, sliced thinly
1 tsp ginger root, minced

3/4 C. grated carrot
salt
pepper
cilantro, to garnish (optional)

Directions

1. In a pot, add the water and rice over high heat and cook until boiling.
2. Set the heat to low and simmer, covered for about 20 minutes.
3. Meanwhile, in a food processor, add the peanuts and pulse until powdered.
4. In a wok, add the butter over medium-high heat and cook until melted completely.
5. Add the onion and stir fry for about 4-6 minutes.
6. Add the carrots, ginger and salt and stir to combine.
7. Set the heat to low and simmer, covered for about 5 minutes.
8. Add the peanuts and black pepper and stir to combine.
9. Transfer the cooked rice into the wok with the vegetable mixture and and gently mix.
10. Enjoy with a topping of the cilantro.

TOMATO FISH
Masala

🥣 Prep Time: 30 mins
🕐 Total Time: 1 hr

Servings per Recipe: 4
Calories	143.6
Fat	7.8g
Cholesterol	0.0mg
Sodium	21.5mg
Carbohydrates	17.6g
Protein	3.3g

Ingredients
900 g kingfish fillets, pat dried, or cod
salt
1/2 tsp chili powder
1/4 tsp turmeric powder
2 tbsp vegetable oil
1 tsp fennel seed
1 tsp mustard seeds
3 onions, chopped

6 cloves garlic, chopped
1/2 inch ginger root, chopped (optional)
2 1/2 tsp cumin powder, divided
6 tomatoes, chopped
1/4 tsp garam masala
2 green chilies, chopped (optional)

Directions
1. In a bowl, add the fish fillets, turmeric, chilli powder and salt and mix well.
2. Refrigerate to marinate for about 30 minutes.
3. In a skillet, add 2 tbsp of the oil and cook over medium heat until heated completely.
4. Add the mustard and fennel seeds and stir fry for bout 30 seconds.
5. Add the onions, ginger and garlic and stir fry for about 1 minute.
6. Stir in the green chili and cumin and stir fry for about 1 minute.
7. Stir in the tomatoes and garam masala and cook until boiling.
8. Set the heat to low.
9. Cover the skillet with the lid and cook for about 15-17 minutes.
10. Set your oven to 350 degrees F.
11. In another non-stick skillet, add some oil and cook until heated completely.
12. Add the fish fillets and cook for about 2 minutes per side.
13. Transfer the fish fillets into a baking dish and top with the tomato mixture evenly.
14. Cook in the oven for about 15 minutes.
15. Enjoy hot

How to Make
Vindaloo

🥣 Prep Time: 1 hr
⏱ Total Time: 1 hr 25 mins

Servings per Recipe: 4
Calories   278.2
Fat   12.8g
Cholesterol   214.5mg
Sodium   1558.7mg
Carbohydrates   15.8g
Protein   25.8g

Ingredients

1 tsp ground turmeric
1 tsp salt
1 tsp fresh ground black pepper
1 tsp red pepper flakes
1 tsp ground coriander
1/2 tsp ground cumin
1/2 tsp dry mustard
1/2 tsp ground cinnamon
1/2 tsp ground ginger
1/4 tsp ground cloves
1/4 tsp ground cardamom
1 1/2 tbsp cider vinegar

3 tbsp vegetable oil
1 large onion, finely chopped
3 cloves garlic, minced
1 (28 oz.) cans tomatoes, drained and finely chopped
1 1/2 lb. large raw shrimp, peeled and deveined
1 tbsp fresh lemon juice
hot cooked rice

Directions

1. In a small bowl, add the vinegar, ground spices and salt and mix until a smooth.
2. In a large pot, add the oil over medium heat and cook until heated completely.
3. Add the garlic and onion and stir fry for about 4-5 minutes.
4. Add the pureed mixture and stir fry for about 20-30 seconds.
5. Stir in the tomatoes and cook until just boiling.
6. Set the heat to low and cook, covered for about 15 minutes, stirring as required.
7. Stir in the shrimp and set the heat to medium.
8. Cook for about 3-4 minutes, stirring as required.
9. Stir in the lemon juice and remove from the heat.
10. Enjoy hot.

CABBAGE
Skillet

Prep Time: 15 mins
Total Time: 30 mins

Servings per Recipe: 7

Calories	122.5
Fat	4.2g
Cholesterol	0.0mg
Sodium	28.1mg
Carbohydrates	19.9g
Protein	3.1g

Ingredients

1 medium cabbage, cored and shredded
2 tbsp vegetable oil
2 - 3 medium potatoes, chopped
1 medium onion, sliced finely
3/4 tsp cumin seed
3/4 tsp mustard seeds
1/2 tsp turmeric powder

1/2 tsp coriander powder
salt
shredded desiccated coconut (optional)
coriander (optional)

Directions

1. In a skillet, add the oil over medium heat and cook until heated through.
2. Add the mustard and cumin seeds and stir fry for about 30 seconds.
3. Add the onion and stir fry for about 4-5 minutes.
4. Add the shredded cabbage, coriander, turmeric and salt and stir to combine.
5. Set the heat to medium-low and cook, covered ufor about 3-4 minutes.
6. Add the potatoes and coconut and stir to combine.
7. Cook until desired doneness of the vegetable, mixing as required.
8. Enjoy with a garnishing of the coriander.

Desi
Caprese Salad Lunch Box

Prep Time: 3 mins
Total Time: 8 mins

Servings per Recipe: 4
Calories	169.7
Fat	13.9g
Cholesterol	0.0mg
Sodium	300.3mg
Carbohydrates	11.5g
Protein	2.0g

Ingredients

1/2 tsp cumin seed
4 tbsp olive oil
2 tbsp balsamic vinegar
1 tbsp lemon juice
2 garlic cloves, minced
1 C. thinly sliced onion rings

4 medium ripe tomatoes, sliced
1 small cucumber, thinly sliced
1/2 tsp ground black pepper
1/2 tsp salt
5 large fresh mint leaves, finely chopped

Directions

1. Place a frying over medium-high heat until heated through.
2. Add the cumin seeds and stir fry for about 25-30 seconds.
3. remove from the heat and place the cumin seeds onto a plate to cool completely.
4. Add the vinegar, lemon juice and oil in a bowl and beat until well combined.
5. In a serving bowl, place the cucumber, tomatoes, onion, garlic, salt and black pepper.
6. Add the vinaigrette, mint and cumin and gently, toss to coat well.
7. Enjoy.

CRANBERRY
Lentil Salad

Prep Time: 10 mins
Total Time: 30 mins

Servings per Recipe: 4
Calories	316.3
Fat	11.0g
Cholesterol	0.0mg
Sodium	799.7mg
Carbohydrates	39.9g
Protein	15.2g

Ingredients

8 oz. dry lentils, rinsed and drained
3 tbsp olive oil
2 tbsp apple cider vinegar
1/2 tbsp maple syrup
1/2 tbsp stone ground mustard
1 tsp salt
1 tsp pepper
1/2 tsp ground cumin
1/4 tsp turmeric
1/4 tsp ground coriander

1/4 tsp ground cardamom
1/8 tsp cayenne pepper
1/8 tsp ground cloves
1/8 tsp ground allspice
1/8 tsp ground cinnamon
1/2 red onion, finely diced
1/2 C. dried cranberries
3 tbsp capers, drained

Directions

1. In a large pan, add the lentils and enough water to cover and cook until boiling.
2. Set the heat to low and cook for about 10-15 minutes.
3. Drain the lentils completely and transfer into a strainer.
4. Immediately, rinse the lentils under running water.
5. For the dressing: in a bowl, add the maple syrup, vinegar, oil, mustard, cumin, turmeric, coriander, cardamom, cayenne pepper, cloves, allspice, cinnamon, salt and black pepper and beat until well combined.
6. In a salad bowl, add the lentils, capers, onions, cranberries and dressing and toss to coat well.
7. Enjoy immediately.

Village Vindaloo II

Prep Time: 15 mins
Total Time: 1 hr 45 mins

Servings per Recipe: 4
Calories   406.8
Fat   18.0g
Cholesterol   145.1mg
Sodium   484.1mg
Carbohydrates   11.9g
Protein   51.6g

Ingredients

2 lb. stewing beef, in 11/2-inch cubes
1 tbsp cumin seed
5 dried red chilies
1 tsp peppercorn
1 tsp fenugreek seeds
6 green cardamom pods (seeds only)
1 tsp black mustard seeds
1/2 tsp salt
1 tsp demerara sugar
5 tbsp white vinegar

2 tbsp oil
1 medium onion, sliced
1 inch fresh ginger, chopped
2 garlic cloves, chopped
2 tsp ground coriander
1/2 tsp turmeric
1/2 pint warm water

Directions

1. In a spice grinder, add the chilis, mustard seeds, fenugreek seeds, cumin seeds, cardamom seeds and peppercorns and grind until powdered.
2. Add the vinegar, sugar and salt and grind until a paste is formed.
3. Place half of the oil in a large pot and cook until heated through.
4. Add the onions and stir fry for about 5-6 minutes.
5. With a slotted spoon, transfer the onion into the spice grinder and grind until a thick paste is formed.
6. Remove the oil from the pot and discard it.
7. In the same pot, add the remaining oil and cook until heated through.
8. Add the beef and sear until no more pink.
9. transfer the beef into a bowl.
10. In the same pot, add the garlic and ginger and stir fry for about 1-2 minutes.

11. Add the turmeric and coriander and stir fry for about 1-2 minutes.

12. Add the spice paste and onion and stir to combine.

13. Set the heat to low and cook for about 4-5 minutes, stirring frequently.

14. Stir in the cooked beef and water and cook, covered until the desired doneness of beef.

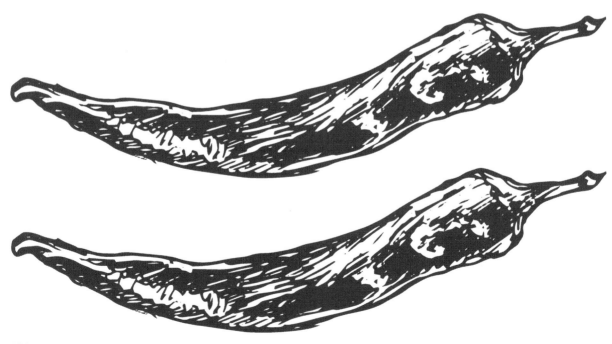

Authentic
Indian Hummus

🍳 Prep Time: 5 mins
🕐 Total Time: 5 mins

Servings per Recipe: 1
Calories	994.0
Fat	44.1g
Cholesterol	0.0mg
Sodium	1324.2mg
Carbohydrates	123.5g
Protein	36.6g

Ingredients

1 can garbanzo beans (plus 1/4 C. of the
bean liquid)
4 tsp lemon juice
1/3 C. tahini
2 tsp cumin
4 -6 cloves garlic, minced
salt and pepper

Directions

1. In a food processor, add all the ingredients and pulse until smooth.

FULL
Vegetarian Stew (Sambaar)

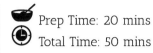

Prep Time: 20 mins

Total Time: 50 mins

Servings per Recipe: 4

Calories	242.0
Fat	1.1g
Cholesterol	0.0mg
Sodium	172.1mg
Carbohydrates	50.8g
Protein	11.8g

Ingredients

1/2 C. tuvar dal
1/2 tsp fenugreek seeds
1 tsp Urad Dal
6 red chilies
1 1/2 tbsp coriander seeds
5 sprigs curry leaves
1/4 coconut, grated
25 - 30 shallots, cleaned and peeled.
1/2 tsp mustards seeds

1 pinch hing
2 green chilies
2 C. chopped vegetables i.e. carrots, green beans, yams
50 ml tamarind pulp
1/4 tsp salt
1 1/2 tsp jiggery, crumbled
oil

Directions

1. In a pan of the water, add the tuvar dal and cook until tender.
2. Drain the dal and transfer into a bowl.
3. With a potato masher, mash the cooked dal.
4. In a nonstick frying pan, add 1 tbsp of the oil and cook until heated completely.
5. Add the fenugreek seeds and stir fry for about 15-20 seconds.
6. Add 1/2 tsp of the urad dal and and stir fry for about 1 minute.
7. Add the coconut, coriander seeds, red chili and 3 sprigs of curry leaves and the grated coconut and stir fry until aromatic.
8. Remove from the heat and keep aside to cool.
9. In a spice grinder, add the spice mixture and a little water and grind until a fine paste is formed.
10. In a skillet, add 1 tbsp of the oil and cook until heated completely.
11. Add the mustard seed and stir fry for about 30 seconds.
12. Add the hing and 1/2 tsp of the urad dal and stir fry for about 1 minute.

13. Stir in the vegetables, onions, remaining curry leaves and green chilis and stir fry for about 2-3 minutes.
14. Add some water and cook, covered until desired doneness of the vegetables.
15. Carefully, extract the pulp from the tamarind ball.
16. In the skillet, add the tamarind pulp, jiggery and salt and cook for about 2-3 minutes.
17. Stir in the mashed dal, spice paste and a little water and cook for until desired doneness.
18. Enjoy hot.

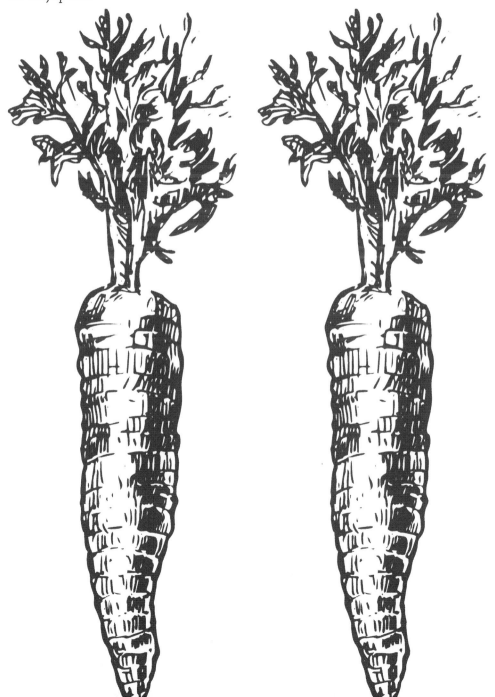

5-INGREDIENT
Tea from Mumbai

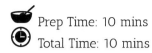

Prep Time: 10 mins
Total Time: 10 mins

Servings per Recipe: 1
Calories	13.6
Fat	0.0g
Cholesterol	0.0mg
Sodium	7.5mg
Carbohydrates	3.4g
Protein	0.0g

Ingredients
1 1/2 C. water
1/2 tsp of crushed ginger
1 tea bag
1/2 tsp honey
milk (optional)

Directions
1. In a pan, add the crushed ginger and water over medium heat and cook until boiling.
2. Cook for about 5-7 minutes.
3. Remove from the heat and through a strainer, strain the water into a mug.
4. In the mug, add the tea bag and stir the honey until dissolved.
5. Enjoy Hot.

Cauliflower
with Homemade Masala

🥣 Prep Time: 10 mins
🕐 Total Time: 30 mins

Servings per Recipe: 6
Calories	130.9
Fat	6.3g
Cholesterol	15.2mg
Sodium	285.1mg
Carbohydrates	15.7g
Protein	5.6g

Ingredients

3 tbsp butter
2 garlic cloves, minced
1/2 tsp ginger
1/2 tsp salt
1/2 tsp turmeric
1/2 tsp cayenne
1/4 tsp cinnamon
1/2 tsp coriander

1/2 tsp mustard seeds
1/2 tsp cumin seed
2 lb. cauliflower, broken into small florets
1/2 C. water
1 1/2 C. fresh peas
2 tbsp cilantro, chopped
2 tomatoes, diced

Directions

1. In a large wok, add the butter over medium heat and cook until melted completely.
2. Add the ginger, garlic and spices and stir fry for about 1 minute.
3. Stir in the cauliflower and water and cook, covered tightly until cauliflower becomes tender.
4. Stir in the peas and cilantro and cook for about 5-7 minutes, mixing occasionally.
5. Stir in the tomatoes and remove from the heat.
6. Enjoy hot.

ASHA'S
Beef Curry

Prep Time: 10 mins
Total Time: 1 hr 40 mins

Servings per Recipe: 4
Calories	204.8
Fat	16.1g
Cholesterol	0.0mg
Sodium	611.2mg
Carbohydrates	15.4g
Protein	3.6g

Ingredients
2 lb. beef steaks, cut in cubes
1 tbsp oil
2 onions, chopped
2 cloves garlic, minced fine
2 green chili peppers, minced fine
1 tbsp fresh grated ginger
1 1/2 tsp turmeric
1 tsp cumin powder

1 tbsp coriander powder
1 tsp salt
1 tsp chili powder
1 (14 oz.) cans chopped tomatoes, with their liquid
1 C. coconut milk

Directions
1. In a skillet, add the oil and cook until heatged through.
2. Add the onions and stir fry for about 4-5 minutes.
3. Add the ginger, garlic, chili peppers, coriander, cumin, turmeric and chili powder and stir fry for about 1 minute.
4. Stir in the beef and cook t about 6-8 minutes.
5. Add the tomatoes and salt and stir combine.
6. Set the heat to low and cook, covered for about 1-1 1/2 hours.
7. Stir in the coconut milk and cook for about 5 minutes.
8. Enjoy hot.

Swiss
Saag

🥘 Prep Time: 5 mins
🕐 Total Time: 25 mins

Servings per Recipe: 4
Calories   265.7
Fat   27.2g
Cholesterol   0.0mg
Sodium   2.5mg
Carbohydrates   6.0g
Protein   0.6g

Ingredients

1 bunch red Swiss chard, cleaned, stems removed and chopped finely
8 tbsp vegetable oil
2 medium onions, minced
2 tbsp vindaloo curry paste

1/2 C. water
2 garlic cloves, minced
2 inches ginger, minced

Directions

1. In a skillet, add the oil over medium-high heat and cook until heated through.
2. Add the onion and stir fry for about 4-5 minutes.
3. Stir in the Swiss chard and cook for about 3-4 minutes.
4. Add the curry paste and stir to combine.
5. Set the heat to low and cook, covered for about 15-20 minutes, mixing as required.
6. Now, set the heat to medium.
7. Stir in the ginger and garlic and cook for about 5 minutes.
8. Enjoy hot.

CAROLINA
Indian Fusion Hash Browns

🥣 Prep Time: 15 mins
🕐 Total Time: 1 hr

Servings per Recipe: 6

Calories	315.5
Fat	7.1g
Cholesterol	0.0mg
Sodium	602.5mg
Carbohydrates	57.8g
Protein	6.8g

Ingredients

6 medium potatoes
4 tbsp water
2 tbsp grated fresh ginger
4 garlic cloves, finely chopped
1 tsp salt
1/2 tsp turmeric

1 pinch ground red pepper
2 tbsp olive oil
1 tsp fennel seed
fresh cilantro (to garnish)

Directions

1. Place the potatoes and enough water to cover in a pan and cook until boiling.

2. Set the heat to low and cook, covered for about 30-35 minutes.

3. Drain the potatoes well and keep aside to cool slightly.

4. Peel the potatoes and then, cut into 1/2-inch cubes.

5. In a food processor, add the garlic, ginger, water, turmeric, red pepper and sat and pulse until smooth.

6. Place the oil in a large heavy-bottomed skillet over medium-high heat and cook until heated completely.

7. Add the fennel seeds and stir fry for about 20-30 seconds.

8. Stir in the spice paste and stir fry for about 1-2 minutes.

9. Stir in the potatoes and stir fry for about 12-15 minutes, flipping as required.

10. Enjoy with a garnishing of the cilantro.

Cardamom
Carrots

Prep Time: 10 mins
Total Time: 25 mins

Servings per Recipe: 4
Calories   94.2
Fat   5.9g
Cholesterol   15.2mg
Sodium   251.1mg
Carbohydrates   10.7g
Protein   0.7g

Ingredients
2 C. carrots, sliced
6 C. cold water
2 tbsp butter
1 tbsp honey
3/4 tsp ground cardamom
1/4 tsp salt

Directions
1. In a pot, add the water and salt and cook until boiling.
2. Add the carrots and cook until just cooked through.
3. Drain the carrots well and keep aside.
4. In a skillet, add the butter over medium heat and cook until melted completely.
5. Stir in the carrots and cook for about 2-3 minutes.
6. Stir in the honey, cardamom and salt and remove from the heat.
7. Enjoy hot.

BEEF
Frezi

Prep Time: 20 mins
Total Time: 1 hr 40 min

Servings per Recipe: 4

Calories	805.6
Fat	59.7g
Cholesterol	198.3mg
Sodium	803.8mg
Carbohydrates	16.4g
Protein	52.8g

Ingredients

1 (400 ml) cans coconut milk
2 lb. lean stewing beef, cut into 2 . 5cm cubes
3 tbsp ghee
2 large yellow onions, sliced and quartered
6 garlic cloves, minced
1 1/2 tsp ginger, minced
1 1/4 tsp ground cumin
1 1/4 tsp coriander, freshly ground
1/2 tsp cayenne pepper

1/4 tsp turmeric
1/4 tsp garam masala
2 green cardamom pods, crushed
2 bay leaves
6 cm cinnamon sticks, broken in half
1 1/2 tbsp tomato paste
1 tsp salt
1 C. plain yogurt
1/2 C. cilantro, chopped

Directions

1. In a Dutch oven, add the coconut milk and cook until boiling.
2. Stir in the beef cubes and set the heat to low.
3. Cook, covered for about 35-40 minutes.
4. With a slotted spoon, transfer the beef cubes and any visible oil in the coconut milk into a bowl.
5. Transfer the coconut milk into a bowl to reserve and with paper towels, pat dry the pan.
6. In the same pan, add the ghee over medium-low heat and cook until melted.
7. Add the garlic, ginger and onion and stir fry for about 3-4 minutes.
8. Transfer the onion mixture into a small bowl.
9. In the same pan, add the cumin, coriander, cayenne pepper, turmeric, garam masala, cardamom pods, cinnamon sticks and bay leaves and stir fry for about 30-40 seconds.
10. Add the tomato paste, cooked beef cubes and reserved coconut milk and cook for about 8-10 minutes, stirring frequently.

11. Stir in the cooked onion, yogurt and salt and cook, covered for about 18-20 minutes.
12. Enjoy with a garnishing of the cilantro.

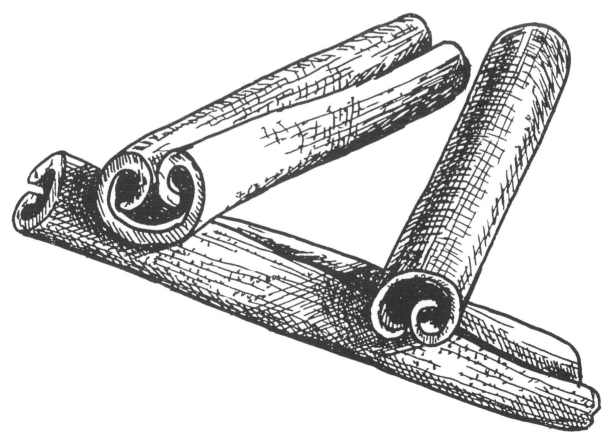

INDIAN HOUSE
Pulao
(Fried Basmati Rice)

Prep Time: 15 mins
Total Time: 45 mins

Servings per Recipe: 6
Calories	393.4
Fat	14.4g
Cholesterol	141.3mg
Sodium	62.4mg
Carbohydrates	55.6g
Protein	11.0g

Ingredients

1 1/2 C. long-grain basmati rice, washed and soaked for 2 hours
1 large onion, thinly sliced
1 large tomatoes, peeled and chopped
4 tbsp oil
1 tbsp ginger-garlic paste
1 tsp cumin powder
2 tsp coriander powder
2 tsp red chili powder

1/4 tsp turmeric powder
1/4 tsp garam masala powder
2 tbsp coconut milk powder
1/2 C. finely chopped coriander leaves
3/4 C. frozen green peas
salt
2 potatoes, quartered and deep fried
4 hard-boiled eggs, shelled

Directions

1. In a heavy bottomed pan, add the oil and cook until heated completely.
2. Add the onion and stir fry for about 4-5 minutes.
3. Add the tomatoes and stir fry for about 2-3 minutes.
4. Add the garlic and ginger paste and stir fry for about 1-2 minutes.
5. Stir in the cumin, coriander, chili powder, turmeric, garam masala and about 2 tbsp of the water and stir fry for about 2-3 minutes.
6. Stir in the peas, coriander, coconut milk, salt and just 2 1/2 C. of the water and cook until boiling.
7. Stir in the rice and simmer, partially covered until all the liquid is evaporated.
8. Set the heat to low and stir in the potatoes.
9. Arrange the eggs on top of the rice mixture and cook, covered for about 8-10 minutes.
10. Enjoy hot.

Mumbai
Deviled Eggs

🥣 Prep Time: 10 mins
🕐 Total Time: 10 mins

Servings per Recipe: 1
Calories	39.3
Fat	2.6g
Cholesterol	93.2mg
Sodium	31.2mg
Carbohydrates	0.4g
Protein	3.1g

Ingredients

6 hard-boiled eggs, shelled and halved
3 1/2 tbsp mayonnaise
3 tbsp minced green onions
1 tbsp minced seeded jalapeño chile

1 1/2 tsp minced mango chutney
1/2 tsp scant garam masala
finely chopped radish, to garnish

Directions

1. Carefully, remove the yolks from the egg halves and transfer into a bowl.
2. With a fork, mash well.
3. Add the mayonnaise, green onions, jalapeño chile, mango chutney, garam masala, salt and pepper and mix well.
4. Stuff the egg whites half with the yolk mixture.
5. Place the chopped radishes. on top if each egg half and enjoy.

SOUTH
Bengali Fish

Prep Time: 5 mins
Total Time: 35 mins

Servings per Recipe: 4
Calories	635.0
Fat	34.6g
Cholesterol	146.2mg
Sodium	258.5mg
Carbohydrates	12.3g
Protein	68.7g

Ingredients
4 salmon fillets
2 onions, chopped
2 garlic cloves, chopped
1 (13 1/2 oz.) cans coconut milk
1 (14 1/2 oz.) cans chopped tomatoes
2 tbsp of garam masala
salt and pepper
olive oil

Directions
1. In a skillet, add 4 tbsp of the olive oil over medium heat and cook until heated through.
2. Add the onions and sauté for 5 minutes.
3. Add the garlic and garam massala and sauté for 5 minutes.
4. Stir in the coconut milk, tomatoes, salt and black pepper and cook, covered for about 20 minutes.
5. Meanwhile, heat another greased skillet and cook the salmon cutlets until desired doneness.
6. Divide the salmon fillets onto serving plates and top with the sauce.
7. Enjoy hot.

Suji Halva
(Rice and Raisin Pudding)

Prep Time: 5 mins
Total Time: 35 mins

Servings per Recipe: 6
Calories   512.0
Fat   21.8g
Cholesterol   50.1mg
Sodium   7.8mg
Carbohydrates   75.6g
Protein   6.0g

Ingredients
2 3/4 C. water
1 1/4 C. sugar
1/2 tsp saffron strand, soaked in 1 tbsp boiling hot milk
140 g unsalted butter

1 1/4 C. semolina (coarse grained)
1/3 C. sliced almonds
1 tsp ground cardamom
1/3 C. sultana

Directions
1. In a large pot, add the soaked saffron, sugar and water over medium heat and cook until sugar is dissolved, mixing continuously.
2. Cook until boiling.
3. Set the heat to low and cover the pan tightly to keep the syrup warm.
4. In another pot, add the butter over low heat and cook until melted completely.
5. Add the semolina, and cook for about 18-20 minutes, gently stirring occasionally.
6. In the last 2 minutes of cooking, stir in the flaked almonds.
7. Now, set the heat under the syrup to medium.
8. Stir in the sultanas and cardamom and cook until boiling,
9. Now, set the heat under the semolina to medium and Stir fry for about 1 minute.
10. Remove the pot of semolina from the heat.
11. Gradually, add the hot syrup into the semolina, mixing continuously.
12. Place the pot over very low heat and cook until all the moisture is absorbed completely, stirring continuously.
13. Now cook, covered for about 5 minutes.
14. Remove from the heat and keep aide, covered for about 5 minutes.
15. Enjoy hot.

INDIAN POTATO WOK
(Khatta Aloo)

🥣 Prep Time: 25 mins

🕐 Total Time: 33 mins

Servings per Recipe: 4

Calories	132.1
Fat	7.2g
Cholesterol	0.0mg
Sodium	8.1mg
Carbohydrates	16.5g
Protein	2.1g

Ingredients

2 tbsp vegetable oil
1/4 tsp ground cumin
1/4 tsp caraway seed
3/4 tsp cumin seed
1/4 tsp ground coriander
1/2 C. finely chopped red onion
3 cloves garlic, minced
1 hot chili pepper, seeded and finely chopped
1 tsp minced fresh ginger

1 tsp turmeric
1 tsp cayenne pepper
1 1/2 C. cooked diced new potatoes
2 tbsp chopped cilantro (fresh coriander)
2 tbsp chopped of fresh mint
1 lime, juiced
salt, to taste
black pepper, to taste

Directions

1. Add the oil in a large wok and cook until heated completely.
2. Add the caraway seeds, cumin seeds, ground cumin and ground coriander and stir fry for about 20-30 seconds.
3. Add the onion and stir fry for about 4-5 minutes.
4. Add the cayenne pepper and turmeric and stir to combine.
5. Stir in the potatoes, lime juice, salt and black pepper and cook until heated completely.
6. Enjoy with the garnishing of the cilantro and mint leaves.

Easy
Flat Bread (Naan)

🥣 Prep Time: 50 mins
🕐 Total Time: 55 mins

Servings per Recipe: 4
Calories   373.8
Fat   7.5g
Cholesterol   54.7mg
Sodium   251.5mg
Carbohydrates   63.3g
Protein   11.7g

Ingredients

2 1/2 C. flour
1/2 tsp baking soda
1/2 tsp baking powder
1/2 C. milk
1/2 C. yogurt

1 tbsp oil
1 beaten egg
1/2 tsp sugar
1/2 tsp cumin seed

Directions

1. In a bowl, add the flour, baking soda, baking powder, sugar and cumin seeds and mix well.
2. In a pan, add the oil an cook until heated completely.
3. In the pan, add the yogurt, milk and egg and cook until just warmed, stirring occasionally.
4. Immediately, remove from the heat.
5. Transfer the milk mixture into the bowl of flour mixture and mix until a dough is formed.
6. Cover the dough and keep aside for about 45 minutes.
7. Set the broiler of your oven.
8. Place the dough onto a floured surface and with your hands, pat into 2 (1/2-inch thick) circles.
9. Arrange the naan onto a baking sheet and cook under the broiler until golden brown from both sides, flipping once.
10. Enjoy hot.

MASALA
Vegetable Cutlets

Prep Time: 20 mins
Total Time: 30 mins

Servings per Recipe: 1

Calories	94.1
Fat	3.8g
Cholesterol	0.0mg
Sodium	63.9mg
Carbohydrates	13.9g
Protein	2.2g

Ingredients

5 oz. green beans (sliced)
2 medium carrots (peeled and grated)
1 slice whole wheat bread, crumbs of
4 oz. new potatoes, boiled until soft
1/2 tsp ginger, grated
1/2 tsp mango powder

1/2 tsp garam masala
1/4 tsp chili powder
4 tbsp cilantro, chopped
salt, to taste
1 tbsp vegetable oil

Directions

1. In a pan of the lightly salted boiling water, add the carrots and green beans and cook, covered for about 8-10 minutes.
2. Drain the carrots and green beans well.
3. In a food processor, add the boiled potatoes, cilantro, breadcrumbs, ginger, mango powder, garam masala, chili powder and salt and pulse until well combined.
4. Make about 3/4-inch sized patties from the mixture.
5. Refrigerate the patties for about 5-10 minutes.
6. In a skillet, add the oil and cook until heated through.
7. Place the patties and cook for about 1-2 minutes.
8. Flip and cook for about 1 minute per side.
9. Enjoy hot.

Indian
Ground Beef Skillet (Kheema)

🍳 Prep Time: 15 mins
⏱ Total Time: 45 mins

Servings per Recipe: 4
Calories   509.9
Fat   12.8g
Cholesterol   73.7mg
Sodium   645.9mg
Carbohydrates   64.8g
Protein   34.7g

Ingredients

1 lb. lean ground beef
1 large onion, chopped
6 garlic cloves, minced
2 tbsp finely minced fresh ginger
salt
1 tsp cumin
1/2 tsp ground cinnamon
1/2 tsp turmeric

1/2 tsp cayenne pepper
1 (10 oz.) packages frozen peas, thawed
2 large potatoes, peeled and cubed
1 (8 oz.) cans tomato sauce
1/2 C. water
1 C. chickpeas, canned, rinsed

Directions

1. Heat a large skillet and sear the beef until browned completely.
2. Drain the grease, leaving 2 tbsp inside the wok.
3. In the same wok, add the ginger, garlic, onion and salt over medium heat and stir fry for about 2-3 minutes.
4. Stir in the cumin, cinnamon, turmeric and cayenne pepper and stir fry for about 1-2 minutes.
5. Stir in the potatoes and peas and cook until boiling.
6. Cook, covered for about 10 minutes.
7. Stir in the chickpeas, tomato sauce and water and cook, covered for about 4-5 minutes.
8. Enjoy hot.

LAMB MASALA
Masala

🥘 Prep Time: 15 mins

🕐 Total Time: 1 hr 25 mins

Servings per Recipe: 4
Calories	771.8
Fat	61.4g
Cholesterol	171.6mg
Sodium	465.3mg
Carbohydrates	12.4g
Protein	41.4g

Ingredients

2 - 3 lb. lamb shoulder, cut in bite sized pieces
2 red onions, chopped
1 tomatoes, chopped
6 garlic cloves, chopped
4 tsp fresh ginger, grated
1 cinnamon stick, 2-inch
1 tsp cumin seed
12 green cardamoms, pods.
1/2 tsp turmeric powder
1 tsp garam masala

1/8 tsp ground allspice
3 bay leaves
1/4 C. chopped cilantro
4 cloves, broken into pieces
1 tsp Indian curry powder
1/2 tsp salt
4 - 6 Serrano chilies, chopped
1 C. plain yogurt
3 tbsp vegetable oil
2 tsp coriander powder

Directions

1. For the marinade: in a large bowl, add the yogurt, ginger, garlic and red chilli powder and mix well.

2. Add the lamb and coat with the marinade generously.

3. Refrigerate to marinate for at least 4 hours or overnight.

4. In a large pan, add the vegetable oil over medium-high heat and cook until heated through.

5. Add the onions, ginger, garlic, bay leaves, cumin seeds, cloves and cinnamon sticks and stir fry for about 6-8 minutes.

6. Remove the lamb from the bowl, reserving marinade.

7. In the pan, add the lamb pieces and stir to combine.

8. Set the heat to medium and cook, covered for about 8 minutes.

9. Remove the lid and stir in the reserved yogurt mixture, Serrano, garam Masala, curry powder, coriander powder, allspice, turmeric and salt.

10. Cook, covered for about 9-10 minutes.
11. Remove the lid and stir the mixture well.
12. Cook, covered for about 12-14 minutes.
13. Stir in the tomatoes and cook, covered for about 9-10 minutes.
14. Add the 1-2 C. of the water and stir to combine.
15. Set the heat to medium and cook, partially covered for about 40-45 minutes.
16. Stir in the cilantro and cook for about 5 minutes.
17. Enjoy hot.

KERALA
Shrimp Curry

Prep Time: 20 mins

Total Time: 35 mins

Servings per Recipe: 4

Calories	544.7
Fat	34.4g
Cholesterol	358.1mg
Sodium	1636.0mg
Carbohydrates	18.8g
Protein	43.8g

Ingredients

3/4 lb. green beans, trimmed, cut into 1 1/2 inch pieces
3 stalks lemongrass
1 C. coarsely chopped fresh cilantro
2/3 C. coarsely chopped shallot
1/4 C. coarsely chopped seeded, jalapeno chile
2 tbsp indian curry powder
1 tbsp coarsely chopped peeled, fresh ginger

1/4 C. coarsely chopped fresh basil, plus sliced leaves for garnish
1/4 C. water
2 tbsp vegetable oil
2 C. canned unsweetened coconut milk
2 1/2 lb. uncooked medium shrimp, peeled, deveined
lime wedge

Directions

1. In a large pan, add the water and salt and bring to a boil.
2. Add the green beans and cook for about 3-4 minutes.
3. Drain the green beans well and keep aside.
4. Cut each lemongrass stalk from the bottom about 2-inch away and then, remove the tops.
5. Now, cut the bottom pieces of each lemongrass stalk into thin slices.
6. In a food processor, add the lemongrass stalk pieces, shallot, ginger, cilantro, chopped basil, jalapeño, curry powder and water and pulse until smooth.
7. In a large skillet, add the oil over medium-high heat and cook until heated completely.
8. Stir in the curry paste and stir fry for about 2-3 minutes.
9. Add the coconut milk and cook until boiling.
10. Add the shrimp and stir to combine.
11. Set the heat to medium-low and cook for about 4-5 minutes.
12. Stir in the green beans and cook until heated completely.
13. Enjoy with a garnishing of the basil alongside the lime wedges.

Lentil Soup
with Fruit Salsa

Prep Time: 20 mins
Total Time: 55 mins

Servings per Recipe: 4
Calories	210.7
Fat	0.7g
Cholesterol	0.0mg
Sodium	105.2mg
Carbohydrates	38.9g
Protein	13.4g

Ingredients
Fruit Salsa:
2/3 C. granny smith apple, finely chopped
1/4 C. celery, finely chopped
1 tbsp fresh cilantro, chopped
1 tbsp fresh lime juice
Lentils:
3 1/2 C. reduced-fat chicken broth
1 C. small dried red lentils
1 C. onion, chopped
1 1/2 C. light coconut milk

3 tbsp tomato paste
1 tsp fresh ginger, peeled grated
1/2 tsp cumin
1/8 tsp turmeric
1 tsp fresh lime juice
salt, to taste
pepper, to taste

Directions
1. For the salsa: in a bowl, add all the ingredients and mix until well combined.
2. Refrigerate, covered to chill before using.
3. In a pot, add the lentils, onion and broth over medium-high heat and cook until boiling.
4. Set the heat to low and cook, covered for about 15-17 minutes.
5. Remove from the heat and stir in the ginger, tomato paste, coconut milk, turmeric and cumin.
6. In a food processor, add the soup mixture in batches and pulse until smooth.
7. In the same pan, add the pureed soup over medium heat and cook, covered for about 10 minutes.
8. Stir in the salt, pepper and lime juice and remove from the heat.
9. Enjoy the hot soup with a topping of the salsa.

APPLE
Cauliflower Stew

Prep Time: 5 mins
Total Time: 25 mins

Servings per Recipe: 6
Calories	100.6
Fat	5.0g
Cholesterol	0.0mg
Sodium	34.2mg
Carbohydrates	13.7g
Protein	2.5g

Ingredients

2 tbsp olive oil
1 C. onion, chopped
1 tart apple, peeled, cored, chopped
1 tbsp curry powder
1 garlic clove

6 C. cauliflower, chopped
4 C. vegetable broth
1 tsp honey
1 tsp apple cider vinegar

Directions

1. In a large pan, add the oil and cook until heated completely.
2. Add he onion and stir fry for about 6-7 minutes.
3. Stir in the garlic, apple and curry powder and stir fry for about 2 minutes.
4. Stir in the broth and cauliflower and cook until boiling.
5. Set the heat to medium-low and cook, covered for about 20 minutes.
6. Remove from the heat and keep aside to cool for about 15-20 minutes.
7. In a food processor, add the soup in batches and pulse until smooth.
8. Return the soup to pan over medium heat.
9. Add the vinegar, honey and salt and stir to combine.
10. Cook until heated through.
11. Enjoy hot.

Mango Kerala Chicken Wings

🥣 Prep Time: 0 mins
🕐 Total Time: 35 mins

Servings per Recipe: 10
Calories   252.5
Fat   19.2g
Cholesterol   84.6mg
Sodium   160.6mg
Carbohydrates   0.9g
Protein   18.1g

Ingredients
4 tsp curry powder
2 tsp ground ginger
1 tsp ground cinnamon
1/4 tsp salt
20 - 24 chicken wings
3 tbsp butter, melted
1 C. mango chutney

Directions
1. In a large bowl, add the cinnamon, curry powder and ginger and mix well.
2. Add the chicken wings and mix well.
3. Refrigerate for at least 3 hours or for whole night.
4. Set your oven to 350 degrees F and line a 15x10x1-inch jelly-roll pan with a piece of foil.
5. Place the chicken wings into prepared pan and coat with the butter.
6. Cook in the oven for about 30-3 minutes.
7. Enjoy hot.

SEAFOOD
Korma

Prep Time: 20 mins
Total Time: 40 mins

Servings per Recipe: 4	
Calories	88.1
Fat	7.3g
Cholesterol	24.1mg
Sodium	123.3mg
Carbohydrates	2.9g
Protein	3.5g

Ingredients
12 large shrimp, peeled and deveined
3 tbsp plain yogurt
1 tsp paprika
1 tsp garam masala
1 - 2 tbsp tomato puree
4 tbsp coconut milk
1 tsp chili powder
3/4 C. water

2 garlic cloves, crushed
1 tsp ginger, grated
1 cinnamon stick, halved
4 cardamom pods
1 tbsp vegetable oil
salt

Directions
1. In a deep dish, add the coconut milk, yoghurt, tomato puree, water, garam masala, paprika, chili powder and salt and mix until well combined.
2. In a skillet, add the oil over low heat and cook until heated through.
3. Add the ginger, garlic, cardamoms and cinnamon and stir fry for about 1 minute.
4. Stir in the yogurt mixture and cook until boiling, mixing occasionally.
5. Stir in the shrimp and cook for about 4-5 minutes.
6. Enjoy with a garnishing of the cilantro.

Curry
Tofu Wok

Prep Time: 10 mins
Total Time: 35 mins

Servings per Recipe: 8
Calories	209.5
Fat	13.4g
Cholesterol	0.0mg
Sodium	317.1mg
Carbohydrates	15.0g
Protein	11.7g

Ingredients

2 lb. firm tofu, cut into 1/2 inch slices
1 tbsp olive oil
2 large onions, peeled and quartered
1 large green pepper, sliced into 2 inch strips
1 tsp crushed garlic
1 tsp ginger, grated
3 tsp curry powder

1 (15 oz.) cans tomato sauce
1 (10 oz.) cans coconut milk
1 tbsp whole cloves
1 tsp cardamom, ground
1 cinnamon stick
salt, to taste
black pepper, to taste

Directions

1. In a large wok, add the oil over medium-high heat and cook until heated through.
2. Add the tofu and stir fry for about 2-3 minute.
3. With a slotted spoon, transfer the tofu onto a plate.
4. In the same wok, add the green pepper and onion and stir fry for about 3-4 minutes.
5. Add the garlic and ginger and stir fry for about 2-3 minutes.
6. Stir in the cooked tofu, coconut milk, tomato sauce, curry powder, cinnamon stick, cardamom, cloves, salt and black pepper and mix well.
7. Set the heat to low and cook for 12-15 minutes, mixing as required.
8. Enjoy hot.

RATATOUILLE
in Bombay

Prep Time: 10 mins
Total Time: 45 mins

Servings per Recipe: 10
Calories	252.2
Fat	19.2
Cholesterol	84.6mg
Sodium	160.6mg
Carbohydrates	0..9g
Protein	18.1g

Ingredients

2 C. diced onions
2 tbsp olive oil
3 cloves garlic, minced
1 fresh chili pepper, minced, seeded for a milder hot
1 tbsp grated fresh ginger root
1 tsp ground cumin
1 tsp ground coriander
1/2 tsp turmeric
1/2 tsp ground cinnamon
1/4 tsp ground cardamom

1 tsp salt
1 pinch of crumbled saffron (optional)
1 C. orange juice
5 C. cubed eggplants, 1 inch cubes
4 C. cubed zucchini
1 1/2 C. diced bell peppers
3 C. diced fresh tomatoes
1/4 C. chopped fresh basil

Directions

1. In a large pan, add the oil and heat over medium heat.
2. Add the onion and cook for about 8-10 minutes, stirring frequently.
3. Add the chili, ginger, garlic, saffron, coriander, cumin, cardamom, cinnamon, turmeric and salt and stir fry for about 1 minute.
4. Stir in the eggplant and orange juice and cook, covered for about 12-15 minutes.
5. Stir in the tomatoes, bell peppers, zucchini and basil and cook, covered for about 12-15 minutes.
6. Enjoy hot.

Kerala
Lunch Box (Raisin Salad)

🥣 Prep Time: 15 mins
🕐 Total Time: 35 mins

Servings per Recipe: 4
Calories   451
Fat   13.7
Carbohydrates   41
Protein   218
Cholesterol   76.9
Sodium   8.3

Ingredients

1 1/2 C. brown rice
4 C. water
1 can asparagus tips, drained
1 red bell pepper, seeded and diced
2 red apples, cored and diced
1/4 C. golden raisins

1/2 C. heavy cream
1 tsp curry powder
1 tsp lemon juice
salt and pepper to taste

Directions

1. In a pot, add the water and rice and cook until boiling.
2. Set the heat to low and cook, covered for 25-30 minutes.
3. Drain any liquid from the rice and keep aside to cool completely.
4. Meanwhile, soak the raisins in water for about 20 minutes.
5. Drain the raisins completely.
6. In a bowl, add the cream and beat until soft peaks are formed.
7. Add the lemon juice, curry powder, salt and black pepper and gently, stir to combine.
8. In another bowl, add the raisins, apples, cooked rice, bell pepper and asparagus and mix.
9. Add the cream mixture and gently, stir to combine.
10. Refrigerate to chill completely before serving.

Manufactured by Amazon.ca
Bolton, ON

24605858R00074